From Great Paragraphs to Great Essays

3

D0223281

GREAT WRITING

FIFTH EDITION

Keith S. Folse

Elena Vestri

David Clabeaux

NATIONAL
GEOGRAPHIC
LEARNING

Australia · Brazil · Mexico · Singapore · United Kingdom · United States

Great Writing 3: From Great Paragraphs to Great Essays
Keith S. Folse, Elena Vestri,
David Clabeaux

Publisher: Sherrise Roehr

Executive Editor: Laura Le Dréan

Director of Global Marketing: Ian Martin

Product Marketing Manager: Tracy Bailie

Senior Director, Production: Michael Burggren

Production Manager: Daisy Sosa

Content Project Manager: Mark Rzeszutek

Manufacturing Planner: Mary Beth Hennebury

Art Director: Brenda Carmichael

Interior Design: Lisa Trager

Cover Design: Lisa Trager

Composition: SPi-Global

Student Edition: 978-0-357-02084-5
Student Edition with Access Code: 978-0-357-02107-1

National Geographic Learning
20 Channel Center Street
Boston, MA 02210
USA

Cengage learning is a leading provider of customized learning solutions with office locations around the globe, including Singapore, the United Kingdom, Australia, Mexico, Brazil, and Japan. Locate our local office at:
www.cengage.com/global

Cengage Learning products are represented in Canada by Nelson Education, Ltd.

Visit NGL online at **ELTNGL.com**

Visit our corporate website at **cengage.com**

Printed in Mexico
Print Number: 04   Print Year: 2022

ii

CONTENTS

CREDITS

Cover © Evgeni Dinev Photography/Moment/Getty Images

Unit 1 Page 2-3: © Bruna Bortolato; Page 5: © Xinhua/Alamy Stock Photo; Page 6: © Don Couch/Barcroft Media/Getty Images; Page 10: © Catherine Karnow/National Geographic Creative; Page 11: © Igor Bulgarin/Shutterstock.com; Page 13: © Ralph Lee Hopkins/National Geograpic Creative; Page 16: © Tim Brown/Alamy Stock Photo; Page 23: © Matthias Hangst/ Getty Images Sport/Getty Images; Page 24: © Warren Faidley/Corbis Documentary/Getty Images; Page 27: © Mark Kostich/ E+/Getty Images; Page 29: © Suwin/Shutterstock.com; Page 31: © MARK THIESSEN/National Geographic Creative

Unit 2 Page 32-33: © Kami/Getty Images; Page 35: © RUKSUTAKARN studio/Shutterstock.com; Page 36: © Minerva Studio/Shutterstock.com; Page 39: © Jan Bures/Shutterstock.com; Page 41: © Louis-Paul st-onge Louis/Alamy Stock Photo; Page 43: © benkrut/iStock/Getty Images; Page 44: © AP Images/Robert Franklin/South Bend Tribune; Page 46: © Roberto Machado Noa/LightRocket/Getty Images; Page 48: © ZUMA Press, Inc./Alamy Stock Photo; Page 50: © Frank Staub/ Photolibrary/Getty Images; Page 54: © Paulo Fridman/Corbis Historical/Getty Images

Unit 3 Page 58-59: © Jean-Pierre Lescourret/Lonely Planet Images/Getty Images; Page 61: © traffic_analyzer/iStock/Getty Images; Page 63: © Annie Griffiths; Page 66: © Martin Novak/Moment/Getty Images; Page 68: © SHENYANG's PHOTO. ALL RIGHTS RESERVED./Moment/Getty Images; Page 70: © Angelo Giampiccolo/Shutterstock.com; Page 71: © Deyana Stefanova Robova/Shutterstock.com; Page 77: © ITAR-TASS News Agency/Alamy Stock Photo; Page 78: © Mimadeo/ Shutterstock.com; Page 81: © Ramin Talaie/Corbis Historical/Getty Images

Unit 4 Page 82-83: © Haggai Matar; Page 86: © mehmettorlak/E+/Getty Images; Page 87: © AFP/Getty Images; Page 89: © kpzfoto/Alamy Stock Photo; Page 94: © Jana Kriz/Moment/Getty Images; Page 99: © Linh Pham/Getty Images News/ Getty Images; Page 103: © Rosanne Tackaberry/Alamy Stock Photo; Page 104: © Leslie Taylo

Unit 5 Page 108-109: © RANDY OLSON/National Geographic Creative; Page 110: © DoctorEgg/Getty Images; Page 112: © Hero Images/Getty Images; Page 120: © Nevada Wier/Getty Images; Page 123: © Christophe Morin/IP3/Getty Images News/Getty Images

Unit 6 Page 132-133: © Powerfocusfotografie/Moment/Getty Images; Page 135: © Chronicle/Alamy Stock Photo; Page 135: © Alexander Spatari/Getty Images; Page 140: © Aerial Archives/Alamy Stock Photo; Page 143: © cyo bo/Shutterstock.com; Page 146: © Ghislain & Marie David de Lossy/Getty Images; Page 151: © Adrian Peacock/Getty Images; Page 152: © Imagine China/Newscom; Page 153: © ESA - European Space Agency & Max-Planck Institute for Solar System Research for OSIRIS Team ESA/MPS/UPD/LAM/IAA/RSSD/INTA/UPM/DASP/IDA

Unit 7 Page 156-157: © GREG MARSHALL/National Geographic Creative; Page 159: © Bruce Leighty - Sports Images/ Alamy Stock Photo; Page 161: © Johan Swanepoel/Alamy Stock Photo; Page 163: © Hero Images/Getty Images; Page 166: © Sean Pavone/Shutterstock.com; Page 167: © Olaf Kruger/imageBROKER/Getty Images; Page 168: © William Berry/ Shutterstock; Page 170: © skynesher/E+/Getty Images; Page 175: © Massimo De Candido/Alamy Stock Photo; Page 176: © Andy Abeyta/Quad-City Times/ZUMA Press, Inc./Alamy Stock Photo

Text Credits: Page 28: © Source: National Geographic. https://news.nationalgeographic.com/2018/04/saving-dying-disappearing-languages-wikitongues-culture/; Page 014: © Source: National Geographic. https://kids.nationalgeographic. com/explore/countries/brazil/#brazil-soccer.jpg; Page 55: © Source: National Geographic. https://news.nationalgeographic. com/future-of-food/future-of-food-agriculture-ecology/; Page 60: © Source: National Geographic. http://natgeo.galegroup. com/natgeo/archive/FeatureArticlesDetailsPage/FeatureArticlesDetailsWindow?disableHighlighting=false&displayGroupNam e=NatGeo-Features&currPage=1&scanId=&query=OQE+%22Aral+Sea%22&docIndex=&source=&prodId=NGMA&search_ within_results=&p=NGMA&mode=view&catId=&u=ngmngma&limiter=&display-query=OQE+%22Aral+Sea%22&displayG roups=&contentModules=&action=e&sortBy=&documentId=GALE%7CKSDWMI194524901&windowstate=normal&acti vityType=BasicSearch&failOverType=&commentary=#pageNo=138; Page 78: © Source: National Geographic. https://www. nationalgeographic.com/travel/destinations/asia/jordan/aqaba-coral-reef-relocation-scuba-activities/; Page 152: © Source: National Geographic. https://relay.nationalgeographic.com/proxy/distribution/public/amp/news/2014/09/140927-largest-cave-china-exploration-science; Page 153: © Source: National Geographic. http://natgeo.galegroup.com/natgeo/archive/ VideosDetailsPage/VideosDetailsWindow?displayGroupName=Videos&currPage=1&query=&prodId=NGMA&source=&p =NGMA&mode=view&catId=GALE%7CPCZCQD796472122&view=docDisplay&total=42&u=ngmngma&limiter=&con tentModules=&displayGroups=&action=e&documentId=GALE%7CDXEULI481118699&windowstate=normal; Page 174: © Source: National Geographic. https://news.nationalgeographic.com/news/2013/07/130720-night-dark-light-pollution-science-stars/?_ga=2.66749804.354764529.1523905109-1019513137.1500397993

GREAT WRITING MAKES GREAT WRITERS

The new edition of *Great Writing* provides clear explanations, academic writing models, and focused practice to help students write great sentences, paragraphs, and essays. Every unit has expanded vocabulary building, sentence development, and more structured final writing tasks.

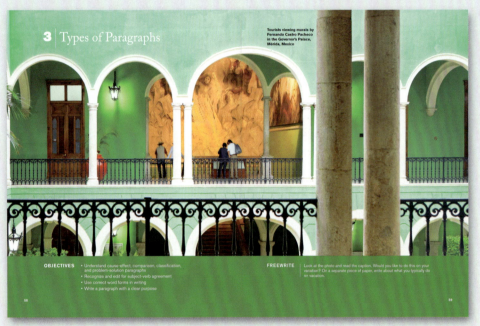

National Geographic images and content spark students' imaginations and inspire their writing.

Each unit includes:

PART 1: Elements of Great Writing teaches the fundamentals of writing.

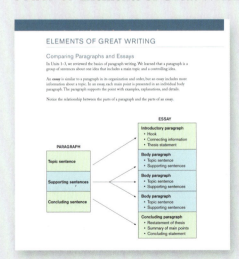

Writing Models encourage students to analyze and use the features of great writing in their own work.

Targeted Grammar presents clear explanations and examples that students can immediately apply to their work.

PART 2: Building Better Vocabulary highlights academic words, word associations, collocations, word forms, and vocabulary for writing.

New Words to Know boxes throughout each unit target carefully-leveled words students will frequently use.

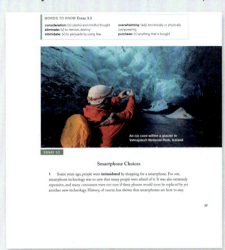

PART 3: Building Better Sentences focuses students on sentence-level work to ensure more accurate writing.

PART 4: Writing activities allow students to apply what they have learned by guiding them through the process of writing, editing, and revising.

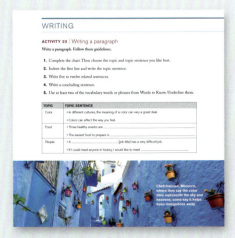

NEW Test Prep section prepares students for timed writing on high-stakes tests.

SUPPORT FOR INSTRUCTORS AND STUDENTS

FOR INSTRUCTORS

The Classroom Presentation Tool brings the classroom to life by including all Student Book pages, answers, and games to practice vocabulary.

Assessment: ExamView™ allows instructors to create custom tests and quizzes in minutes. **ExamView™** and **Ready to Go Tests** are available online at the teacher companion website for ease of use.

FOR STUDENTS

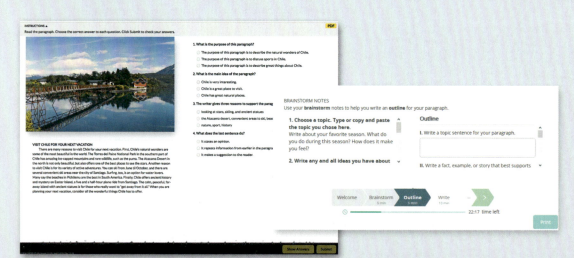

The Online Workbook provides additional practice in vocabulary, grammar, and writing, plus remediation activities for students who have not mastered at-level vocabulary and grammar.

NEW Guided online writing practice reinforces the writing process, helping students become stronger and more independent writers.

ACKNOWLEDGEMENTS

The Authors and Publisher would like to acknowledge and thank the teachers around the world who participated in the development of the fifth edition of *Great Writing*.

ASIA

Anthony Brian Gallagher, Meijo University, Nagoya

Atsuko Aoki, Aoyama Gakuin University, Tokyo

Atsushi Taguchi, Okayama University of Science, Imabari Campus, Ehime

Helen Hanae, Reitaku University, Kashiwa

Hiroko Shikano, Juchi Medical University, Gotemba

Hisashi Shigematsu, Toyo Gakeun University, Tokyo

Jeremiah L. Hall, Meijo University, Nagoya

Jian Liang Fu, Kwansei Gakuin University, Nishinomiya

Jim Hwang, Yonsei University, Asan

John C. Pulaski, Chuo University and Tokyo Woman's Christian University, Tokyo

Junyawan Suwannarat, Chiang Mai University, Chiang Mai

Katherine Bauer, Clark Memorial International High School, Chiba

Kazuyo Ishibashi, Aoyama Gakuin Univeristy, Tokyo

Lei Na, Jump A-Z, Nanjing

Lor Kiat Seng, Southern University College, Seremban

Mark McClure, Kansai Gaidai Univeristy, Osaka

Matthew Shapiro, Konan Boys High School, Ashiya

Nattalak Thirachotikun, Chiang Mai University, Chiang Rai

Nick Boyes, Meijo University, Nagoya

Nick Collier, Ritsumeikan Uji Junior and Senior High School, Kobe

Olesya Shatunova, Kanagawa University, Yokohama

Pattanapichet Fasawang, Bangkok University International College, Bangkok

Paul Hansen, Hokkaido University, Sapporo

Paul Salisbury, Aichi University, Nagoya

Randall Cotten, Gifu City Women's College, Gifu

Sayaka Karlin, Toyo Gakuen University, Tokyo

Scott Gray, Clark Memorial International High School Umeda Campus, Osaka

Selina Richards, HELP University, Kuala Lumpur

Terrelle Bernard Griffin, No. 2 High School of East China Normal University-International Division, Shanghai

William Pellowe, Kinki University, Fukuoka

Yoko Hirase, Hiroshima Kokusai Gakuin University, Hiroshima

Youngmi Lim, Shinshu University, Matsumoto

Zachary Fish, RDFZ Xishan School AP Center, Beijing

USA

Amanda Kmetz, BIR Training Center, Chicago, Illinois

Amy Friedman, The American Language Institute, San Diego, California

Amy Litman, College of Southern Nevada, Las Vegas, Nevada

Angela Lehman, Virginia Commonwealth University, Richmond, Virginia

Aylin Bunk, Mount Hood Community College, Portland, Oregon

Barbara Silas, South Seattle College, Seattle, Washington

Bette Brickman, College of Southern Nevada, Las Vegas, Nevada

Breana Bayraktar, Northern Virginia Community College, Fairfax, Virginia

Carolyn Ho, Lone Star College-CyFair, Cypress, Texas

Celeste Flowers, University of Central Arkansas, Conway, Arkansas

Christina Abella, The College of Chicago, Chicago, Illinois

Christine Lines, College of Southern Nevada, Las Vegas, Nevada

Clare Roh, Howard Community College, Columbia, Maryland

DeLynn MacQueen, Columbus State Community College, Columbus, Ohio

Eleanor Molina, Northern Essex Community College, Lawrence, Massachusetts

Emily Brown, Hillsborough Community College, Florida

Emily Cakounes, North Shore Community College, Medford, Massachusetts

Erica Lederman, BIR Training Center, Chicago, Illinois

Erin Zoranski, Delaware Technical Community College, Wilmington, Delaware

Eugene Polissky, University of Potomac, Washington, DC

Farideh Hezaveh, Northern Virginia Community College, Sterling, Virginia

Gretchen Hack, Community College of Denver, Denver, Colorado

Heather Snavely, California Baptist University, Riverside, California

Hilda Tamen, University of Texas Rio Grande Valley, Edinburg, Texas

Holly Milkowart, Johnson County Community College, Overland Park, Kansas

Jessica Weimer, Cascadia College, Bothell, Washington

Jill Pagels, Lonestar Community College, Houston, Texas

Jonathan Murphy, Virginia Commonwealth University, Richmond, Virginia

Joseph Starr, Houston Community College, Southwest, Houston, Texas

Judy Chmielecki, Northern Essex Community College, Lawrence, Massachusetts

Kate Baldridge-Hale, Valencia College, Orlando, Florida

Kathleen Biache, Miami Dade College, Miami, Florida

Katie Edwards, Howard Community College, Columbia, Maryland

Kenneth Umland, College of Southern Nevada, Las Vegas, Nevada

Kevin Bowles, Linfield College, McMinnville, Oregon
Kim Hardiman, University of Central Florida, Orlando, Florida
Kori Zunic, San Diego City College, San Diego, California
Kris Lowrey, Virginia Commonwealth University, Richmond, Virginia
Kristin Homuth, Language Center International, Oak Park, Michigan
Leon Palombo, Miami Dade College, North Campus, Miami Beach, Florida
Lily Jaffie-Shupe, Virginia Polytechnic Institute, Blacksburg, Virginia
Lisse Hildebrandt, Virginia Commonwealth University, Richmond, Virginia
Luba Nesterova, Bilingual Education Institute, Houston, Texas
Madhulika Tandon, Lone Star College, University Park, Houston, Texas

Matthew Wolpert, Virginia Commonwealth University, Richmond, Virginia
Megan Nestor, Seattle Central College, Seattle, Washington
Meredith Kemper, University of Central Arkansas, Conway, Arkansas
Mike Sfiropoulos, Palm Beach State College, Lake Worth, Florida
Milena Eneva, Chattahoochee Technical College, Atlanta, Georgia
Myra M. Medina, Miami Dade College, Miami, Florida
Naomi Klimowicz, Howard Community College, Columbia, Maryland
Nicholas C. Zefran, Northern Virginia Community College, Springfield, Virginia
Nicole Ianieri, East Carolina University, Greenville, North Carolina
Patricia Nation, Miami Dade College, Miami, Florida

Paul Kern, Green River College, Auburn, Washington
Rachel DeSanto, Hillsborough Community College, Tampa, Florida
Ramon Perez, Northern Virginia Community College, Dumfries, Virginia
Rebecca McNerney, Virginia Commonwealth University, Richmond, Virginia
Richard Roy, Middlesex County College, Edison, New Jersey
Sandra Navarro, Glendale Community College, Glendale, California
Shane Dick, College of Southern Nevada, Las Vegas, Nevada
Sheila Mayne, University of Pennsylvania, Philadelphia, Pennsylvania
Stephen Johnson, Miami Dade College, Florida
Sumeeta Patnaik, Marshall University, Huntington, West Virginia
Summer Webb, International English Center, Colorado

Tom Sugawara, University of Washington, Seattle, Washington
Viviana Simon, Howard Community College, Columbia, Maryland
William Albertson, Drexel University, Philadelphia, Pennsylvania
Yu Bai, Howard Community College, Laurel, Maryland

MIDDLE EAST
Deborah Abbott, Prince Muhammad Bin Fahd University, Al Khobar, Saudi Arabia
Genie Elatili, Prince Muhammad Bin Fahd University, Al Khobar, Saudi Arabia
Julie Riddlebarger, Khalifa University, United Arab Emirates
Karla Moore, Virginia International Private School, Abu Dhabi, United Arab Emirates
Laila AlQadhi, Kuwait University, Kuwait

FROM THE AUTHORS

Great Writing began in 1998 when three of us were teaching writing and frequently found ourselves complaining about the lack of materials for English language learners. A lot of books talked about writing but did not ask the students to write until the end of a chapter. In essence, the material seemed to be more of a lecture followed by "Now you write an essay." Students were reading a lot but writing little. What was missing was useful sequenced instruction for developing ESL writers by getting them to write.

Each of us had folders with our own original tried-and-true activities, so we set out to combine our materials into a coherent book that would help teachers and students alike. The result was *Great Paragraphs* and *Great Essays*, the original books of the *Great Writing* series. Much to our surprise, the books were very successful. Teachers around the world reached out to us and offered encouragement and ideas. Through the past four editions we have listened to those ideas, improved upon the books, and added four more levels.

We are proud to present this 5th edition of the *Great Writing* series with the same tried-and-true focus on writing and grammar, but with an added emphasis on developing accurate sentences and expanding level-appropriate academic vocabulary.

We thank those who have been involved in the development of this series over the years. In particular for the 5th edition, we would like to thank Laura Le Dréan, Executive Editor; the developmental editors for this edition: Lisl Bove, Eve Einselen Yu, Yeny Kim, Jennifer Monaghan, and Tom Jefferies. We will be forever grateful to two people who shaped our original books: Susan Maguire and Kathy Sands-Boehmer. Without all of these professionals, our books would most definitely not be the great works they are right now.

As always, we look forward to hearing your feedback and ideas as you use these materials with your students.

Sincerely,

Keith Folse
April Muchmore-Vokoun
Elena Vestri
David Clabeaux
Tison Pugh

1 | Paragraphs

National Geographic Explorer Albert Yu-Min Lin stands in Upper Antelope Canyon in Arizona, USA. Millions of years of water erosion carved this narrow space out of Navajo sandstone.

FREEWRITE Look at the photo and read the caption. National Geographic Explorer Albert Lin has traveled from the remote highlands of Mongolia to the jungles of Guatemala, always seeking to learn more. On a separate piece of paper, write what it means to explore.

ELEMENTS OF GREAT WRITING

Paragraphs and Topic Sentences

A **paragraph** is a group of sentences about a central idea. A paragraph has a clear purpose, such as to list, to show causes or effects of something, or to argue a point. Every part of a paragraph has a specific function, and every part is important. The three main parts of a paragraph are:

- the topic sentence
- the supporting sentences
- the concluding sentence

The **topic sentence** tells the reader the main idea or thought that the writer is trying to express. It is a one-sentence summary of the entire paragraph. Other sentences in the paragraph help to develop the idea presented in the topic sentence. The organization of a paragraph is based on the topic sentence.

The two main elements of a topic sentence are the **topic** or main subject of the paragraph and the **controlling idea**. The controlling idea guides the main subject in the direction that the writer wants to take it. Study the following examples of topic sentences.

Supercomputers are used to perform very complex tasks.
      topic   controlling idea

From this sentence, we know that the paragraph is going to discuss supercomputers. Specifically, it will discuss some complicated tasks of supercomputers.

Computers have changed enormously in the past 10 years.
      topic   controlling idea

This topic sentence tells us that the paragraph is going to explain how computers have changed.

Different **computers** can appeal to different people.
         topic   controlling idea

From this topic sentence, we know that the paragraph is going to explain the characteristics of different computers that appeal to different kinds of people.

Computers were invented in the 20th century.
       topic

The information in this sentence is a simple fact. This is not a good topic sentence because it does not indicate that there is anything more to say about the topic. It does not have a controlling idea that a writer can discuss in a paragraph.

Researcher Song Zhongwei and a colleague study dinosaur fossils on display at Chongqing Museum of Natural History in Chongqing, Southwest China.

ACTIVITY 1 | Selecting a good topic sentence

For each pair of sentences, check (✓) the better topic sentence. Be prepared to explain your choices.

1. _____ **a.** A person who is interviewing for a job should arrive on time to the interview.

✓ ___✓___ **b.** A person who is interviewing for a job should do three important things during the interview.

✓ **2.** ___✓___ **a.** Smartphones have many useful features for communication.

_____ **b.** Smartphones are often used to send text messages.

3. _____ **a.** Fossils are the remains of plants or animals that died a long time ago.

✓ ___✓___ **b.** There are numerous techniques that scientists use to discover the age of a fossil.

✓ **4.** ___✓___ **a.** There are many theories about who killed John F. Kennedy.

_____ **b.** John F. Kennedy was assassinated on November 22, 1963.

5. ___✓___ **a.** Online dictionaries can help students in two important ways.

_____ **b.** Online dictionaries are available in numerous languages.

ACTIVITY 2 | Studying the topic sentence of a paragraph

Read the paragraph and answer the questions that follow.

> **WORDS TO KNOW** Paragraph 1.1
>
> **discovery:** (n) the finding of something new
> **investigate:** (v) to research, carefully examine
>
> **lead to:** (v phr) to result in
> **throughout:** (prep) in all parts of

Types of Explorers

Throughout history, explorers have been inspired to **investigate** land, space, and sea. One type of explorer is the land explorer. Land explorers travel great distances through rough wilderness[1] in the hopes of making a great **discovery**. An example of a historical land explorer is Sacagawea. She was a Native American guide and translator who helped lead the Lewis and Clark Expedition from 1804 to 1806. Her journey with Lewis and Clark helped to open new routes from the Mississippi River to the Pacific Ocean. Another type of explorer is the space explorer. Space explorers include the astronauts, astronomers, and engineers who investigate outer space[2]. Neil Armstrong, who, in 1969, became the first person to walk on the moon, is an excellent example of a space explorer. Finally, ocean explorers dive deep into the sea, looking for answers to unsolved mysteries. Jacques Cousteau (1910–97) of France was one of the most famous undersea explorers in modern times. He was an oceanographer, a researcher, and an award-winning filmmaker. In addition, his inventions **led to** better scuba diving equipment. Although these explorers have answered many of nature's mysteries, there is still much to learn. Tomorrow's explorers are sure to answer more of these questions.

[1]wilderness: land in its natural state
[2]outer space: area where the planets and stars are

National Geographic Explorer Dr. Guillermo de Anda explores a cenote near the Mayapan Ruins in Yucatan, Mexico.

1. Underline the topic sentence.

2. What is the controlling idea of this paragraph?

   _____ inspired to investigate land, space, sea. _____

3. How many types of explorers are discussed in this paragraph? __4__

4. Check (✓) the statement that tells the purpose of the paragraph.

   __✓__ **a.** to explain why exploration is important

   _____ **b.** to describe space exploration

   _____ **c.** to discuss types of explorers

   _____ **d.** to show why being an explorer is an excellent career

Five Features of a Good Topic Sentence

A well-written topic sentence has certain features:

1. **It guides the whole paragraph.** It lets the reader know what the rest of the paragraph will be about.

2. **It is not a well-known fact.** A good topic sentence is not a general fact that everyone accepts as true. For example, *Most cars use gasoline* is not a good topic sentence because there is not much more to say about the topic.

3. **It is specific.** *Credit cards are useful* is not a good topic sentence because it is too general. The reader does not know exactly what to expect in the paragraph. *Credit cards are useful on international trips* is a more effective topic sentence because it is specific. The paragraph will most likely explain how credit cards can be used in one particular situation—an international trip.

4. **It is not too specific.** *Credit cards were invented in 1950.* This sentence is too specific as a topic sentence. There is nothing else to say. It could be a supporting sentence in a paragraph about the history of credit cards, but not a topic sentence.

5. **It includes a controlling idea.** A controlling idea is a word or phrase that helps guide the flow of ideas in the paragraph: *A credit card is one of the most important things that a traveler needs while on vacation.* The underlined words in this sentence are the controlling idea. The reader expects to read why or how a credit card is important on a vacation.

ACTIVITY 3 | Recognizing effective topic sentences

Read each of the following sets of sentences. Write the topic and check (✓) the best topic sentence.

1. Topic: _____

_____ **a.** The air conditioner is one of the most useful inventions of the 20th century.

_____ **b.** Large air conditioners can be very expensive.

_____ **c.** Portable air conditioners can be easily moved from room to room.

2. Topic: _____

_____ **a.** Jobs in biomedical engineering do not pay as much as those in electrical engineering.

_____ **b.** Biomedical engineering is a fast-growing industry.

_____ **c.** Biomedical engineers invent prosthetic devices for people with disabilities.

3. Topic: _____

_____ **a.** Snowboarding is a winter sport.

_____ **b.** Few people know the interesting history of snowboarding.

_____ **c.** Snowboards are made of fiberglass and have sharp metal edges.

Controlling Ideas

The **controlling idea** in a topic sentence guides the paragraph and lets the reader know what the paragraph is going to be about. The topic of the paragraph is limited by the controlling idea—it narrows the topic.

Here are some examples of topic sentences. The topics are boldfaced, and the controlling ideas are underlined.

1. **E-books** are easier to use than print books.

   The reader expects to learn what makes e-books easier to use.

2. **Singapore** is a very popular vacation destination.

   The reader expects to learn some reasons why Singapore is a popular vacation destination.

3. There are three things to be aware of before **swimming in the ocean.**

   The reader expects to learn about the three things to know before swimming in the ocean.

ACTIVITY 4 | Identifying topic sentences and controlling ideas

Read each set of sentences. Check (✓) the best topic sentence. Underline the controlling idea in the sentence you choose.

1. _____ **a.** Europeans drink far more coffee than people from other parts of the world.

   _____ **b.** Coffee is more bitter in Europe than in other countries.

   _____ **c.** Most Europeans drink coffee in order to wake up in the morning.

2. _____ **a.** Roller coasters are frightening.

   _____ **b.** Roller coaster safety has improved tremendously over the last 200 years.

   _____ **c.** Roller coasters are called "Russian Mountains" in many languages.

3. _____ **a.** Over one million U.S. high school athletes participated in outdoor track-and-field events last year.

   _____ **b.** The sport of track-and-field began in 770 BC.

   _____ **c.** The sport of track-and-field has increased in popularity in recent years.

ACTIVITY 5 | Using controlling ideas to narrow a topic

The following topic sentences are too general. Rewrite them, and add to or change the controlling ideas.

1. Lying is bad.

   _____

2. It is important to work hard.

   _____

3. The Eiffel Tower is located in Paris, France.

   _____

WRITER'S NOTE Indenting

When you write a paragraph, remember to indent the first sentence. This placement is typically about a half inch (1.3 cm) from the left margin.

➡ Singapore is a very popular vacation destination in Asia. There are several reasons why tourists love this area.

ACTIVITY 6 | Writing topic sentences

Read the three paragraphs and write a topic sentence for each one. Be sure each topic sentence includes a controlling idea.

> **WORDS TO KNOW** Paragraphs 1.2 to 1.4
>
> **appreciate:** (v) to understand the value or importance of something
> **beneficial:** (adj) good; helpful
> **category:** (n) a type, kind
> **cause:** (v) to make something happen
> **function:** (v) to work, perform a task
> **lack:** (v) to have too little of something, be without
>
> **occur:** (v) to happen, take place
> **process:** (n) general way of doing something
> **recommendation:** (n) written or spoken praise; approval
> **regardless of:** (prep) no matter
> **tend to:** (v phr) to be likely to do something

PARAGRAPH 1.2

_____

_____

First, breakfast gives the body fuel to change into energy. This is an important way to start the day after not eating all night long. Without that morning meal, the body may **lack** the necessary fuel for energy. In addition, perhaps the most **beneficial** effect of eating breakfast is that digesting[1] food "wakes up" the body's metabolism—the chemical activity required for the body to **function** properly. When a person is asleep, metabolism slows down. Eating breakfast **causes** the metabolism to increase in the morning. Finally, eating breakfast also reduces hunger later in the morning. An individual who does not eat breakfast **tends to** eat too much at lunch. It is no surprise that people have been saying for generations that "breakfast is the most important meal of the day."

[1]digest: to process food in the stomach

A family eats Sunday breakfast.

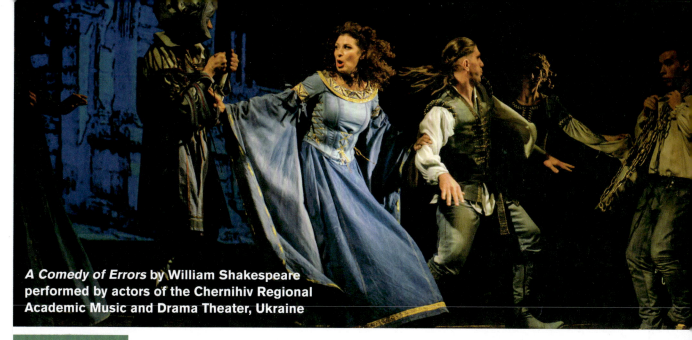

A Comedy of Errors by William Shakespeare performed by actors of the Chernihiv Regional Academic Music and Drama Theater, Ukraine

PARAGRAPH 1.3

Stage acting, which is the oldest form of acting, **occurs** in front of a live audience, in places ranging from large performance halls to small theaters. The next and probably the most well-known **category** of acting is television acting. This type of acting is for weekly programs that are produced in a TV studio. The third and final type of acting is film acting for a movie. Film acting is similar to TV acting, but the process is more complex, and it takes longer to make a movie. **Regardless of** the type of acting, audience members **appreciate** actors for the many hours of enjoyment they provide.

PARAGRAPH 1.4

Perhaps the best solution is to take advantage of job-search websites. Most of these services are free for job seekers to use. After a job seeker sets up an account, it is easy to search for a particular type of job within an industry. Additionally, these online sites can store important documents. With a quick click of the mouse, job seekers can upload items such as résumés[1], letters of **recommendation**, etc. Because this information is saved on the website, the application **process** is much easier. Without a doubt, the use of job-search websites is an efficient solution for job seekers.

[1]résumé: a written work history

Titles

A **title** tells you what you will find in a book, a movie, a story, or a text. The title is usually very short, and it is not usually a sentence. A good title has something that catches the reader's interest, but it does not tell everything about what the paragraph or essay will say.

ACTIVITY 7 | Writing titles

With a partner, write two possible titles for each paragraph. Then compare your best titles with your classmates.

1. Paragraph 1.2 **a.** _Breackfast and heath._

b. _why eating breakfast is important._

2. Paragraph 1.3 **a.** _Type of acting._

b. _Acting._

3. Paragraph 1.4 **a.** _____

b. _the way of taking advantage by searching job_

Brainstorming

Brainstorming is quickly writing down all the thoughts that come into your head about a topic. When you brainstorm, you do not think about whether each idea is good or bad, or whether your writing is correct. You simply write down as many ideas as possible in a few minutes. The process is called *brainstorming* because it feels like there is a storm of ideas in your brain.

ACTIVITY 8 | Brainstorming

Choose one of the topics. First, brainstorm ideas about your topic on a separate piece of paper. Write at least four ideas. Then write a topic sentence for a paragraph about your topic. Be sure to include a controlling idea.

- Types of friends
- How online learning is changing education
- Why some movies are so popular
- A person who changed my life
- Benefits of studying English
- The effects of fame on a person

Topic sentence: _____

_____

ACTIVITY 9 | Writing your own paragraph

Use your brainstorming notes and topic sentence from Activity 8 to write a paragraph on a separate piece of paper. Be sure that the controlling idea in your topic sentence guides the whole paragraph.

Supporting Sentences

Supporting sentences describe, explain, clarify, or give examples of the main idea in the topic sentence. They answer questions such as *Who? What? When? Where? Why?* and *How?*

Each paragraph must have enough supporting details to make the main idea clear to the reader. In addition, each supporting sentence should be closely related to the topic sentence and its controlling idea. Study the following examples.

1. Topic sentence: Hunters kill elephants for their valuable ivory tusks, and they must be stopped.

   Supporting sentence: In fact, approximately 50 elephants are killed in Africa every day.

2. Topic sentence: Automobile insurance has a number of benefits, including emergency towing service.

   Supporting sentence: A quick phone call is all it takes to have the broken-down car taken to a mechanic.

3. Topic sentence: Cell phones allow parents to stay in better contact with their children.

   Supporting sentence: As long as a child's cell phone is turned on, a parent can reach a child at any time.

Types of Supporting Sentences

Experienced writers use many different kinds of supporting sentences. Supporting sentences can:

1. **Explain**
   Topic sentence: There are many support services for students at the university.
   Supporting sentence: Since many college students experience at least some level of stress, counselors are always available to help them.

2. **Describe**
   Topic sentence: The Platte River is an extremely important area for migratory birds such as sandhill cranes.
   Supporting sentence: This rich, natural environment provides the birds with a safe place to rest before continuing on their lengthy journey.

Sandhill cranes taking flight from the water in New Mexico, USA

3. **Give reasons**
   Topic sentence: Note taking is one of the most useful study skills to learn.
   Supporting sentence: Reviewing good notes before a test will help students learn the
                         most important information.

4. **Give facts**
   Topic sentence: Jogging is not as easy as it appears.
   Supporting sentence: More than 20 percent of adults cannot run farther than 100 meters
                         without stopping to rest.

5. **Give examples**
   Topic sentence: Brazil has several key natural resources.
   Supporting sentence: Brazil is a leading producer of cocoa, sugarcane, and soybeans.

WRITER'S NOTE Supporting Details

One way to develop supporting details is to ask questions about your topic sentence. Look at
your topic sentence and ask questions with *Who? What? When? Where? Why?* or *How?*

ACTIVITY 10 | Using questions to write supporting details

For each topic sentence, write two questions that the supporting sentences could answer.

1. Some pesticides should not be used on vegetable crops.

   What kinds of pesticides should not be used? Why should we avoid using pesticides?

2. Many coffee producers are committed to using environmentally friendly farming methods.

   why many coffee producere need to use them?
   How does it work/by using evironmentally friendly
             in earth   farming methods?

3. Although snow skiing and water skiing seem very different, the two sports have some
   similar characteristics.

   what's the similar btween snow sking & water skiing?

4. Trophy hunting, in which people pay for the opportunity to hunt endangered animals, is
   controversial.

   _____

   _____

5. Children who participate in extracurricular activities are often more confident than those
   who do not.

   _____

   _____

Avoiding Unrelated Sentences

Some writers include too many ideas in one paragraph. Remember that a paragraph should focus on just one controlling idea, the one in the topic sentence. Every sentence must support the topic sentence. In this way, supporting sentences help maintain the unity of the paragraph. Sentences with unrelated ideas should be removed.

ACTIVITY 11 | Identifying unrelated sentences

Read the two paragraphs. For each numbered sentence, check (✓) if it is a *good* supporting sentence or an *unrelated* sentence. Be prepared to explain your answer. (Note that neither paragraph has a concluding sentence at this point. Concluding sentences will be added in Activity 17.)

> **WORDS TO KNOW** Paragraphs 1.5 to 1.6
>
> **characteristic:** (n) a special quality **maintain:** (v) to keep in good condition
> **entire:** (adj) complete; whole **massive:** (adj) huge

PARAGRAPH 1.5

The Features of a Successful Restaurant

Regardless of the type of food they serve, all successful restaurants have similar **characteristics**. First, these restaurants provide fast and friendly service, with servers who are polite at all times. They make sure that customers' needs are met throughout the meal. [1] Since customers are choosing to eat out, obviously the quality of the food is also important. A good restaurant always uses the freshest ingredients in its dishes. [2] Some of the best-quality cheeses can be imported from France. [3] Finally, good restaurants also have a pleasant atmosphere. They are clean and well **maintained**, and they also pay attention to details such as decor[1] and lighting.

[1]decor: style; design

	Good	Unrelated
Sentence 1	☐	☐
Sentence 2	☐	☐
Sentence 3	☐	☐

An exhibit shows the African influence on American arts and music at the National Museum of African American History and Culture, Washington, DC.

PARAGRAPH 1.6

Visiting Washington, DC

There are two types of popular tourist attractions in Washington, DC: the museums and the monuments. [1] The most interesting museums in Washington, DC, are the 16 Smithsonian museums. There is a museum for every interest, from the Museum of African American History and Culture to the Air and Space Museum. A tourist can easily spend an **entire** week visiting these 16 museums, which all have free admission. Washington, DC, also has very beautiful memorials[1] and monuments. One of the most frequently visited is the Lincoln Memorial. This memorial is home to a **massive** statue of President Abraham Lincoln and an engraved[2] copy of Lincoln's famous speech, the Gettysburg Address. [2] There are many food trucks there, so it is a good place to have lunch. Close by is the Washington Monument. [3] This magnificent stone tower was built in memory of the first president of the United States, George Washington. It is beautiful in its simple design.

[1]memorial: a monument dedicated to the memory of the dead
[2]engraved: carved into stone or wood

	Good	Unrelated
Sentence 1	☐	☐
Sentence 2	☐	☐
Sentence 3	☐	☐

Grammar: Sentences vs. Fragments

Every sentence in English must have a subject and verb and a complete idea.* A sentence without a subject or verb in the main clause is called a **fragment**. The word *fragment* means a piece of something.

*The one exception is the imperative, as in *Look at the Burj Khalifa*. In an imperative, the subject is understood as *you*.

FRAGMENTS	SENTENCES
Cheetahs and gazelles enemies.	Cheetahs and gazelles **are** enemies.
Wheat grown in Argentina.	Wheat **is** grown in Argentina.
Is a lot of pollution today.	**There** is a lot of pollution today.
Maya Angelou a famous author.	Maya Angelou **is** a famous author.
The Burj Khalifa the tallest building in the world.	The Burj Khalifa **is** the tallest building in the world.
Because the engine failed.	Because the engine failed, **the pilot had to make an emergency landing**.

ACTIVITY 12 | Checking for fragments

Read the sentences. The subject in each clause is underlined. If the subject has a verb, write *C* (correct) and circle the verb. If a verb is missing, write *F* (fragment) and add a verb in the correct place.

_F_ **1.** Students _{encounter} an incredible amount of new vocabulary in English every day.

_____ **2.** Some learners this problem by using flash cards.

_____ **3.** What are flash cards?

_____ **4.** How do language learners use them?

_____ **5.** A flash card a small card for learning vocabulary.

_____ **6.** Learners write the new word on one side of the card.

_____ **7.** Then they a definition on the other side.

_____ **8.** Students test themselves on the vocabulary words by guessing the meaning and then checking the answer.

_____ **9.** Because learners create their own cards, they can focus on words that are important for them.

_____ **10.** Even though it a traditional method, using flash cards extremely useful.

Grammar: Count and Non-Count Nouns

There are two kinds of nouns: **count** and **non-count**. If you can count a noun (*five sandwiches, nine ideas*), then it has a singular form (*sandwich, idea*) and a plural form (*sandwiches, ideas*); it is a count noun. If you cannot count a noun (*pollution, art, hair*), it is a non-count noun and generally has only one form.

Some adjectives are used only with plural nouns. When writing, check to make sure nouns after these adjectives are count and plural.

a few months	**numerous** cases	**several** people	**those** blogs
many reasons	**other** decisions	**these** methods	**two** tests

A common error is to forget to use the plural form of the noun as in the example below:

Many scientist_s attended the recent meeting in Seoul. At that meeting, there were several

presentation_s about the numerous effect_s of climate change.

ACTIVITY 13 | Editing for noun forms

Look at the underlined nouns in each sentence. If there is an error in noun form, make a correction above the word. If the sentence is correct, write *C* next to it.

1. More than 65 million <u>family</u> in the United States face the daily challenges of taking care of their <u>elders</u>.

2. It is only logical that this <u>number</u> will grow in the future as the <u>population</u> soars.

3. Many <u>people</u> who take care of their parents or other family <u>member</u> work at a regular job all day.

4. About 40 percent of those who care for their <u>elder</u> also take care of their own children.

5. Over 70 percent of caregivers are women, and nearly one-third of these <u>woman</u> are over the age of 65.

6. Amazingly, eight out of ten caregivers provide care for an average of four <u>hour</u> a <u>day</u>, seven <u>days</u> a week.

7. Caregivers can often experience problems with their own <u>healths</u>, finances, and jobs.

8. Therefore, it is extremely important for people who care for their elders to also take the <u>times</u> to care for themselves.

Supporting Details

In a paragraph, supporting details, such as examples, reasons, descriptions, or facts, support the topic sentence. Remember: Answering questions about the topic sentence (*Who? What? When? Where? Why?* or *How?*) is a good way to generate details in a paragraph.

ACTIVITY 14 | Asking the right questions

Choose one of the topics below and write a topic sentence. Then write questions about the topic sentence using the appropriate question words. If you cannot think of at least three questions, perhaps your topic sentence is weak.

- An important moment in a person's life
- A famous person who is popular today
- Good study habits
- An easy sport

1. Topic sentence: *One of the most important days in a person's life is his or her wedding day.*

   Who? *Who is involved in the event?*

   What? *What generally happens?*

   When? *When does this event happen?*

   Where? *Where does this event happen?*

   Why? *Why is it considered an important day?*

   How? *How do the bride and groom feel at the time?*

2. Topic sentence: _____

   _____

   Who? _____

   _____

   What? _____

   _____

   When? _____

   _____

   Where? _____

   _____

   Why? _____

   _____

   How? _____

   _____

ACTIVITY 15 | Writing supporting sentences

Look at your topic sentence and questions from Activity 14. Write supporting sentences that answer each question that you wrote.

1. _____

   _____

2. _____

   _____

3. _____

   _____

4. _____

   _____

5. _____

   _____

6. _____

   _____

ACTIVITY 16 | Writing a paragraph

Use the topic sentence from Activity 14 and the supporting sentences from Activity 15 to write a paragraph on a separate piece of paper. Be sure to use only supporting sentences that relate to the topic sentence and its controlling idea.

Concluding Sentences

The **concluding sentence** concludes, or ends, a paragraph. A concluding sentence has three main features:

1. It is usually the last sentence of a paragraph.
2. It lets the reader know that the paragraph has ended.
3. It brings the paragraph to a logical conclusion. It can do this by:

   a. Restating the **main idea** of the topic sentence, as in Paragraph 1.4:

   Without a doubt, the use of job-search websites is an efficient solution for job seekers.

   b. Offering a **suggestion**, giving an **opinion**, or making a **prediction**, as in Paragraph 1.1:

   Tomorrow's explorers are sure to answer more of these questions. (prediction)

Transitions with Concluding Sentences

Here is a list of transitional words and phrases that are commonly used at the beginning of concluding sentences. Note that each is followed by a comma.

As a result	Clearly	In conclusion	Overall
Because of this	For these reasons	In the end	Therefore
Certainly	For this reason		

Examples:

In conclusion, successful businesses are the result of the actions of good workers.

Overall, buying a used car has more advantages than buying a new car.

For more information on connectors and transitions, see the *Writer's Handbook*.

ACTIVITY 17 | Writing concluding sentences

Go back to Paragraph 1.5, "The Features of a Successful Restaurant," and Paragraph 1.6, "Visiting Washington, DC." Write a concluding sentence for each paragraph. Use a different transition and type of concluding sentence for each one. Check (✓) what each concluding sentence does.

1. Paragraph 1.5

Topic: Restaurants

_____

_____

What does the concluding sentence do?

☐ restates the main idea ☐ offers a suggestion

☐ gives an opinion ☐ makes a prediction

2. Paragraph 1.6

Topic: Washington, DC

_____

_____

What does the concluding sentence do?

☐ restates the main idea ☐ offers a suggestion

☐ gives an opinion ☐ makes a prediction

Three Features of a Well-Written Paragraph

A well-written paragraph has three key features.

1. **It has a topic sentence that states the main idea**. The topic sentence lets the reader know what the paragraph will be about. It contains the topic and a controlling idea. When it is the first sentence of a paragraph, it needs to be indented.

2. **All of the sentences are about one topic**. Each sentence of the paragraph relates to and supports the topic sentence and its controlling idea. Focusing on one topic helps to maintain the coherence or logical flow of the paragraph.

3. **The last sentence, or concluding sentence, brings the paragraph to a logical conclusion.** Sometimes the concluding sentence is a restatement of the topic sentence. At other times, writers offer a suggestion, opinion, or prediction based on their purpose.

ACTIVITY 18 | Analyzing a paragraph

Read the paragraph and answer the questions that follow.

> **WORDS TO KNOW** Paragraph 1.7
>
> **appeal:** (v) to satisfy, interest   **rely on:** (v phr) to depend on
> **overall:** (adv) in general; considering everything

PARAGRAPH 1.7

The Popularity of the Summer Olympic Games

Why is it that, every four years, people from all over the world stop to watch the Summer Olympic Games? There are many reasons for their popularity. First of all, there are sporting events that **appeal** to almost every sports fan. From track-and-field[1] to swimming and soccer (football), fans can **rely on** continuous entertainment for approximately two weeks. In the Winter Olympics, one of the most popular sports is ice skating. In addition, viewers get to watch the best athletes from all over the world compete against each other. Finally, the athletes compete for their own countries and flags, and Olympics fans get to support and cheer them on. When athletes receive a medal for their country, they feel a great sense of pride. Fans share the feeling as they count the number of medals their country wins. **Overall**, this competition is one of the most popular sporting events in the world.

[1]track-and-field: sporting events that involve running and jumping and throwing

Eliud Kipchoge of Kenya winning gold in the men's marathon at the 2016 Olympic Games, Rio de Janeiro, Brazil

1. What is the purpose of this paragraph? Begin your sentence with *The purpose of* ...

   Why every 4 years people from all over the world stop to watch sumer Olympic game.

2. Underline the topic sentence.

3. What is the controlling idea?

   3 reasons for popularity

4. Underline the concluding sentence. Is the concluding sentence a restatement, a suggestion, an opinion, or a prediction? _____

5. Cross out the sentence that does not belong. Why does it not belong?

   In the winter ~~~~~~ ice skating.

6. What suggestion do you have to improve this paragraph?

   _____

   _____

ACTIVITY 19 | Bringing it all together

Read the paragraph and underline the topic sentence. Then cross out the sentence that is not a good supporting sentence. Write a concluding sentence for the paragraph.

WORDS TO KNOW Paragraph 1.8

disaster: (n) a sudden event that causes destruction, catastrophe

predict: (v) to say what will happen in the future

PARAGRAPH 1.8

Two Natural Disasters

Although tsunamis and hurricanes can both cause a lot of damage and result in **disaster**, they are each very different. For one, tsunamis are formed by natural events such as landslides, eruptions from volcanoes, and, most typically, underwater earthquakes[1]. Hurricanes, on the other hand, are powerful storms that form over warm ocean water. The two storms also differ in how they are **predicted**. Tsunamis can only be predicted about an hour in advance at most, while storms that can become hurricanes can be carefully followed by meteorological[2] technology weeks in advance. As a result, people can more easily prepare for a hurricane than they can for a tsunami. Tsunamis are very frightening. Finally, tsunamis occur in the Pacific Ocean. Hurricanes, which are called by different names depending on where they form, can develop in any ocean.

_____

_____

[1]earthquake: violent movement of Earth's surface
[2]meteorological: relating to Earth's atmosphere or weather

A hurricane strikes a coast line.

BUILDING BETTER VOCABULARY

ACTIVITY 20 | Word associations

Circle the word or phrase that is more closely related to the bold word on the left.

1. appeal	dislike	like
2. appreciate	expensive	thankful
3. beneficial	good	bad
4. category	shape	type
5. cause	make happen	take away
6. discovery	find	search
7. function	feel	perform
8. lack	have a lot of	not have enough of
9. massive	big	small
10. overall	in addition	in general

ACTIVITY 21 | Collocations

Fill in the blank with the word or phrase that most naturally completes the phrase.

characteristic	disaster	investigate	regardless of	rely on

1. _____ a crime

2. a natural _____

3. _____ a dictionary

4. _____ the consequences

5. a unique _____

6. give a job _____

7. _____ a delicious dinner

8. _____ make careless errors

9. a very efficient _____

10. _____ the night

ACTIVITY 22 | Word forms

Complete each sentence with the correct word form. Use the correct form for nouns and verbs.

NOUN	VERB	ADJECTIVE	ADVERB	SENTENCES
category	categorize			**1.** There are four _____ of news stories. **2.** The graduate students had to _____ the samples.
		entire	entirely	**3.** The city of Pompeii was _____ destroyed in AD 79. **4.** The Transantarctic Mountains stretch across the _____ continent of Antarctica.
maintenance	maintain			**5.** Regular car _____ will help you avoid costly repairs. **6.** Good firefighters must _____ their calm in the face of a disaster.
occurrence	occur			**7.** World War II _____ between the years of 1939 and 1945. **8.** There was one major _____ of the Spanish flu in the 20th century.
prediction	predict	predictable		**9.** The company's financial _____ is risky. **10.** Nostradamus _____ numerous events many years ago.

ACTIVITY 23 | Vocabulary in writing

Choose five words from Words to Know. Write a complete sentence with each word.

1. _____

2. _____

3. _____

4. _____

5. _____

BUILDING BETTER SENTENCES

WRITER'S NOTE Editing Abbreviations

Your teacher may use these abbreviations when marking your writing.

cap = capitalization error   *s/p* = singular-plural error   *wf* = word form error

frag = fragment   *s/v agr* = subject-verb agreement

ACTIVITY 24 | Editing from teacher comments

Read the teacher's comments. Then make the corrections.

PARAGRAPH 1.9

Baby three-toed sloth in a rain forest in Costa Rica

Amazing Sloths

Sloths amazing animals that live in Central and *frag* south America. *cap*

These animals are well known for their laziness. Scientists believe that

their slow movement helps them escape from predators—animals

that might hurt them. Because many predator *s/p* have sharp eyesight,

they are looking for animals that movement *wf* quickly. When sloths sees *s/v agr*

a predator, they actually move more slowly, hoping that they will

disappear into the background. For sloths, being slowly *wf* has its rewards.

Combining Sentences

Short sentences create an uneven writing style. Longer sentences connect ideas, and this makes it easier for the reader to understand.

Study these sentences. The important information is circled.

(Susan) (went) to (the mall.)

Susan (wanted to buy) a (new sweater.)

The sweater was (for Susan's mother.)

The most important information from each sentence can be used to create longer, more coherent sentences. Both of these sentences are good ways to combine the shorter sentences:

Susan went to the mall because she wanted to buy a new sweater for her mother.

Susan wanted to buy a new sweater for her mother, so she went to the mall.

ACTIVITY 25 | Combining sentences

Read the sentences for each item, and circle the most important information. Combine the ideas into one sentence. You may change the word forms, but do not change or omit any ideas. There may be more than one answer.

1. Drinks are harmful to the teeth.
The drinks are sugary.
Children have teeth.

_____

_____

2. Drones can be used for fun.
Drones can be used for exploration.
Drones can be used for advertising.

_____

_____

3. The United Nations maintains peace.
The peace is international.
The United Nations helps countries.
The countries need aid.
The aid is humanitarian.

_____

_____

ACTIVITY 26 | Writing about a photo

On a separate piece of paper, write five to eight sentences about the photo. Make sure that every sentence uses the correct singular or plural form of the noun. Avoid fragments by checking for subjects and verbs in each sentence.

A farmer uses a drone to spray fertilizer on corn fields.

WRITING

ACTIVITY 27 | Writing a paragraph

Choose one of the topics below. Follow these steps to write a paragraph:

- smart phones
- friendships
- job interviews
- a good meal

1. Brainstorm ideas on a separate piece of paper.

2. Start your paragraph with a topic sentence that includes a clear controlling idea. Indent this first sentence.

3. Add supporting sentences that relate to the controlling idea in the topic sentence. Use the questioning strategy to generate ideas for these supporting details.

4. End with a concluding sentence.

If you need ideas for wording, see *Useful Words and Phrases* in the *Writer's Handbook*.

Peer Editing

Experienced writers proofread their work and rewrite it several times. Before you revise your writing, it is helpful to let someone else read it, offer comments, and ask questions to clarify your meaning. You may not always see your own mistakes, but a reader can help you see where you need to make improvements.

Peer editing is an easy way to get feedback about your paper. In this method, another student (a peer) reads your paper and makes comments using a set of questions and guidelines. Comments from a peer can help you strengthen areas in your paragraph that are weak or that appear confusing to the reader.

Here are some suggestions for peer editing:

1. **Listen carefully.** It is important to listen carefully to comments and suggestions about your writing. Remember that the comments are about the writing, not about you.

2. **Make helpful comments.** When you read a classmate's paper, choose your words and comments carefully. For example, instead of saying "This is bad grammar," or "I can't understand any of your ideas," make helpful comments, such as "You need to make sure that every sentence has a verb," or "What do you mean in this sentence?"

3. **Read, read, read!** It is important for you to understand why a piece of writing is good or is not good, and the best way to do this is to read, read, and read some more. The more writing styles you become familiar with, the better your writing can become, too.

ACTIVITY 28 | Peer editing

Exchange papers from Activity 27 with a partner. Read your partner's paragraph. Then use Peer Editing Form 1 in the *Writer's Handbook* to help you comment on your partner's paragraph. Consider your partner's comments as you revise your paragraph.

Additional Topics for Writing

Here are five topics for a paragraph. Follow your teacher's instructions and choose one or more topics to write about.

TOPIC 1: Look at the photo at the beginning of this unit. Write a paragraph about an impressive natural or man-made location in your country.

TOPIC 2: Write a paragraph about the differences between two popular types of household pets.

TOPIC 3: Discuss the problem of overcrowding in a large city that you are familiar with, and offer some possible solutions.

TOPIC 4: Write a paragraph about two or three different study methods. Be sure to include a definition or description of each of the methods.

TOPIC 5: Compare the difference between a vacation in the mountains and a vacation by the beach.

TEST PREP

You should spend about 25 minutes on this task. Write about the following topic:

Explain what firefighters do. What different responsibilities do they have? What kinds of things do firefighters do every day? What are the dangers of this job?

Include any relevant examples from your knowledge or experience. Remember to include a topic sentence, supporting details, and a concluding sentence. Check your writing for sentence fragments. Write at least 150 words.

A firefighter works on a burning hillside in Montana, USA.

2 | Features of Good Writing

Young men perform a dance in the Middle East.

OBJECTIVES
- Understand purpose, audience, clarity, unity, and coherence
- Use clear, descriptive language
- Use clear pronoun reference
- Write a paragraph and use proofreading strategies to check it

ELEMENTS OF GREAT WRITING

Five Features of Good Writing

In Unit 1, you learned the basic parts of a paragraph:

- a topic sentence with a controlling idea
- supporting sentences
- a concluding sentence

Now that you are familiar with these key components of a paragraph, the next step is to consider how the sentences interact with each other and how your reader will relate to your paragraph.

In this unit, you will learn five features of writing:

1. purpose
2. audience
3. clarity
4. unity
5. coherence

Feature 1: Purpose

When we talk about the **purpose** of a paragraph, we are talking about the reasons that a writer is writing a particular paragraph. Writers must understand their purpose in order to keep their writing focused. The purpose is the goal the writer is trying to achieve.

Some of the most common goals of academic writing are:

- to explain
- to persuade
- to summarize or retell
- to describe

ACTIVITY 1 | Analyzing a paragraph

Discuss the questions. Then read the paragraph and answer the questions that follow.

1. Why are bees important to us?
2. *Extinct* means that an animal no longer exists or lives on Earth. What animals have become extinct? What caused their extinction?

> **WORDS TO KNOW** Paragraph 2.1
>
> **alternative:** (n) another choice
> **decline:** (n) a lowering of numbers, prices, etc.
> **permanent:** (adj) lasting forever or for a long time
>
> **poison:** (n) a substance that can cause illness or death in a living organism
> **significantly:** (adv) by a large amount
> **substance:** (n) a particular kind of matter or material

Honey bees collecting pollen in springtime

The Dangers of a Declining Bee Population

Bee populations across the world have dropped **significantly**, and this is a serious problem. These insects play a very important role in food supply because they pollinate[1] fruits and vegetables. Without bees to pollinate plants, food will be extremely difficult to produce. One of the biggest causes of this **decline** in bee populations is pesticides[2]. Bees come in contact with the **poison** and either die immediately or, even worse, carry it back to the beehive where it could cause **permanent** damage. A long-term solution is for farmers and gardeners to find **alternatives** to the dangerous pesticides that are used on their crops and gardens. Many natural **substances**, such as oil and soap sprays, can do the same job as chemical products. In addition, beehives can be placed closer to food crops. The less distance a bee has to travel, the less chance there is of its injury or death since bees have very fragile wings. Whichever action is chosen, something needs to be done now to prevent bees from becoming extinct.

[1]pollinate: to transfer pollen to a plant so that it can reproduce
[2]pesticide: a chemical used to kill pests and insects

1. What is the purpose of this paragraph? Begin your sentence with *The purpose of ...*

_____

_____

2. What is the topic sentence? Write it and circle the controlling idea.

_____

_____

3. Reread the paragraph. What two solutions are offered to the problem of the declining bee population?

_____

_____

Purpose Statement

A **purpose statement** is a short sentence that clearly defines the point of the paragraph. Writers often create a purpose statement before they begin writing.

Purpose statements are written by the writer for the writer. If, for example, you are going to write a paragraph about subtitles in TV shows, your purpose statement might be:

> The purpose of this paragraph is to list the benefits of subtitles in TV programs.

By referring to your purpose statement as you write, you will be less likely to start writing about the history of television subtitles or the different types of subtitles.

Remember: The purpose statement is not the same as the topic sentence, which is usually the first sentence in a paragraph. The purpose statement is *not* included in the paragraph.

Here are some sample topics and possible purpose statements:

TOPIC	PURPOSE STATEMENTS
Driving in the rain	1. The purpose of this paragraph is to list the dangers of driving in the rain. 2. The purpose of this paragraph is to propose solutions to the dangers of driving in the rain.
Insufficient sleep	1. The purpose of this paragraph is to explain the negative effects of not getting enough sleep. 2. The purpose of this paragraph is to offer solutions for insomnia.
Tornadoes	1. The purpose of this paragraph is to describe how tornadoes are formed. 2. The purpose of this paragraph is to compare tornadoes and water spouts.

A tornado in the American plains

ACTIVITY 2 | Writing purpose statements

Read each of the following topics. Think of what you would write about the topic and why.
Then write two purpose statements for each topic.

1. Topic: Fast food

   Purpose statement 1: *The purpose of this paragraph is to give reasons for the popularity of fast-food restaurants.*

   Purpose statement 2: *The purpose of this paragraph is to argue that there are negative effects of eating fast-food.*

2. Topic: Sources of energy

   Purpose statement 1: _____

   _____

   Purpose statement 2: _____

   _____

3. Topic: An important invention

   Purpose statement 1: _____

   _____

   Purpose statement 2: _____

   _____

4. Topic: Friendships

   Purpose statement 1: _____

   _____

   Purpose statement 2: _____

   _____

5. Topic: Study habits

   Purpose statement 1: _____

   _____

   Purpose statement 2: _____

   _____

Feature 2: Audience

The second feature of writing is to keep your **audience**, your readers, in mind as you write. Ask yourself: How much background knowledge does the audience have? Is there any background information that should be added to the paragraph? Is formal or informal language more appropriate?

WRITER'S NOTE Academic Writing

Academic writing usually requires formal language. This includes using the third person (*he, she, it, the mayor, scientists*) and avoiding idioms, informal language, and contractions.

Feature 3: Clarity

Clarity refers to how easy it is for the reader to understand your writing. Writers need to explain their points clearly. Clear sentences are not vague or indirect; they get the point across to the reader by using specific, concise, and direct language.

Here are two ways that you can improve clarity:

- Use clear and descriptive language
- Use clear pronoun reference

Using Clear and Descriptive Language

Clear and descriptive language improves clarity in a paragraph. It helps the reader accurately see the person or thing the writer is describing. There are two ways to do this:

1. **Avoid nondescriptive words,** such as *thing* and *happy*. Instead choose more specific words when the context allows.

EXAMPLES	EXPLANATION
✗ Usain Bolt of Jamaica set the world record for the 100-meter dash in 2009 at 9.58 seconds. This is an exceptional <u>thing</u>.	**Thing** is a poor word choice in this context because it is not descriptive.
✓ Usain Bolt of Jamaica set the world record for the 100-meter dash in 2009 at 9.58 seconds. This is an exceptional **achievement**.	**Achievement** is a better word choice because it is more precise. Other descriptive words that could fit in this sentence are: **feat** or **accomplishment**.
✗ The survivors were <u>happy</u> to see the rescue team.	**Happy** is not a good word choice because it does not give a clear idea of how the survivors felt.
✓ The survivors were **relieved** to see the rescue team.	**Relieved** expresses a more precise feeling. Other descriptive words that could fit in this sentence are: **ecstatic** or **elated**.

A panther chameleon in Madagascar

2. **Add details in sentences.** Sentences with details are more interesting and informative to read. The following nondescriptive sentences have been revised to show more clarity.

NONDESCRIPTIVE LANGUAGE	DESCRIPTIVE LANGUAGE
The man went to work.	My neighbor, Mr. Andrews, went to work at the power plant every day for 25 years.
Chameleons are lizards.	Color-changing chameleons are lizards that are found mainly in Madagascar.
The explorers crossed the river.	The tired explorers slowly crossed the raging river.

ACTIVITY 3 | Choosing more precise words

Write three alternative words that are more descriptive or precise than the adjectives or adverbs given. Use a dictionary or thesaurus if needed.

1. good   _wonderful_   _incredible_   _delightful_

2. bad   _____   _____   _____

3. very   _____   _____   _____

4. big   _____   _____   _____

5. interesting   _____   _____   _____

6. nice   _____   _____   _____

ACTIVITY 4 | Writing descriptive phrases

Rewrite each phrase to make it more descriptive.

1. the old house _____

2. the long road _____

3. a nice gift _____

4. the big mountain _____

5. a very difficult exam _____

ACTIVITY 5 | Rewriting for clarity

Rewrite each sentence with more descriptive words and details.

1. That person knows a lot about computers.

_____

_____

2. His clothes looked nice.

_____

_____

3. Tokyo is big.

_____

_____

4. The company made changes.

_____

_____

5. The team won the championship.

_____

_____

ACTIVITY 6 | Analyzing a paragraph

Read the paragraph and answer the questions that follow.

> **WORDS TO KNOW** Paragraph 2.2
>
> **device:** (n) an electrical or mechanical machine
> **interfere:** (v) to interrupt a situation
> **release:** (n) allowing something that was held back to go
>
> **signal:** (v) to send a message
> **stimulate:** (v) to increase activity

PARAGRAPH 2.2

Electronic Devices and Sleep

Although many people enjoy using their "smart **devices**" before going to bed, these habits can actually make it more difficult to fall asleep. At a time when a person should be relaxing and getting ready for sleep, being online, reading posts on social media sites, or watching TV can be too **stimulating**. Instead of relaxing the mind, these activities can make the average person feel more awake. In addition, scientific researchers have found that using electronic devices in the hours before sleep **interferes** with the **release** of sleep hormones[1]. This is because such devices give off an artificial blue light, which **signals** the brain to stay awake. For a restful night's sleep, experts recommend turning off electronic devices at least one hour before bedtime. If people can follow this guideline, they will most certainly enjoy a deeper and more restful sleep.

[1]hormone: a chemical in the body that stimulates activity

1. What is the purpose of this paragraph? Begin your sentence with *The purpose of...*

_____

_____

2. In the topic sentence, circle the topic and underline the controlling idea.

3. Underline the concluding sentence. What type of concluding sentence is it?

☐ restatement   ☐ suggestion   ☐ opinion   ☐ prediction

Grammar: Clear Pronoun Reference

Pronouns take the place of nouns. Pronouns can improve your writing as long as every pronoun refers to a specific noun.

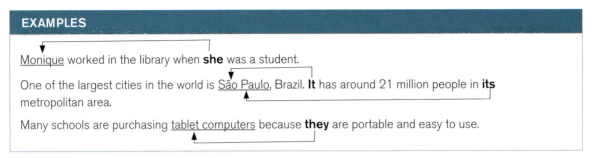

EXAMPLES

Monique worked in the library when **she** was a student.

One of the largest cities in the world is São Paulo, Brazil. **It** has around 21 million people in **its** metropolitan area.

Many schools are purchasing tablet computers because **they** are portable and easy to use.

Notice the unclear pronoun reference in the following sentence:

> Students should consistently focus on their homework from the time they are in primary school. **They** say that this habit increases intellectual ability. (Who does *they* refer to?)

To clarify, rewrite the sentence with the precise noun:

> **Most educational experts** say that this habit increases intellectual ability.

ACTIVITY 7 | Editing for clear pronoun reference

Circle the pronouns. If the pronoun reference is not clear, rewrite the sentence.

1. Blueberries and grapefruit are both healthy snacks loaded with vitamins. They are considered "superfoods" because of their many health benefits.

   Blueberries and grapefruit are considered "superfoods" because of their many health benefits.

2. Sushi is a Japanese food made with raw fish. They consider it one of the most popular types of Japanese food.

3. Marine biologists study animals that live in the ocean, including whales, sharks, and octopuses. They are the biggest creatures on Earth.

4. Scientists use electronic devices to follow animals such as wolves and bears. They want to study the animals' habits in the wild.

5. Environmentalists are concerned about the increasing number of wildfires in the last few years. They have become more widespread because of environmental changes.

ACTIVITY 8 | Revising for clear pronoun reference

Read the comparison paragraph. Note the five underlined pronouns, which are not clear. Then follow the directions on the next page.

> **WORDS TO KNOW** Paragraph 2.3
>
> **major:** (adj) main; (one of the) most important   **unlike:** (prep) different from
> **on average:** (phr) usually, normally

PARAGRAPH 2.3

The Weather in Chicago and Miami

Both Chicago and Miami are very popular cities, but their climates[1] could not be more different. The first difference is the seasons. Chicago has all four seasons, but Miami does not. People in Chicago enjoy very different weather in the summer, fall, winter, and spring. **1** <u>It</u>, in contrast, has only two seasons: a very mild winter and a very long summer. Another **major** difference in the weather between these two cities is that **2** <u>its</u> worst weather occurs in the winter. **On average**, the high temperature reaches only around 32 degrees Fahrenheit (0 degrees Celsius), and the low each night goes down to about 20 degrees (-7 degrees Celsius). **Unlike** Chicago, the problem in **3** <u>it</u> is not the cold but rather the heat. In the summer, the daytime temperature reaches 95 degrees (35 degrees Celsius) and drops to only 75 (24 Celsius) or so at night. Finally, **4** <u>they</u> worry about different weather problems. While a blizzard[2] is the biggest fear for residents of Chicago, the biggest weather problem for **5** <u>them</u> is a hurricane. In sum, these two cities experience very different weather.

[1]climate: the type of weather that a region has
[2]blizzard: a severe snowstorm

View of downtown Chicago, Illinois, on a winter morning

Replace the unclear pronouns from Paragraph 2.3 with precise nouns.

1. It: _____

2. its: _____

3. it: _____

4. they: _____

5. them: _____

Grammar: Consistent Pronoun Reference

Writers should not jump from singular to plural when referring to the same noun. They should also avoid shifting among first, second, and third person unless it is necessary to do so.

✗ **A child** needs to interact with others in order to form social relationships. Without this contact, <u>children</u> will not develop normally.

✓ **A child** needs to interact with others in order to form social relationships. Without this contact, **the child** will not develop normally.

✗ **Parents** should teach children how to express feelings. <u>We</u> can do this by sharing <u>our</u> own feelings.

✓ **Parents** should teach children how to express feelings. **They** can do this by sharing **their** own feelings.

Children play a game together in a physical education class.

ACTIVITY 9 | Revising for consistent pronoun usage

The following sentences change person and/or number within the sentence, causing unnecessary shifts. Change the incorrect pronouns and any verb forms that need to change.

1. Before students choose a major, she should always speak to an academic advisor.

2. One should carpool if you want to save on gas.

3. Doctors warn people that you should watch the kind of food you eat every day.

4. The population of the United States has grown steadily over the past century, and they continue to grow.

5. Alligators and crocodiles are distinct in that it is either a freshwater or saltwater reptile.

6. It is important for a company to respond quickly to problems we may face.

7. Many computer users hate software updates because of the interruption to our work.

ACTIVITY 10 | Editing a paragraph

There are six errors in pronoun usage. Find and correct the errors and any verb forms that need to change as a result.

PARAGRAPH 2.4

A Fast-Growing Industry

Biomedical engineering is one of the fastest-growing segments of the tech industry. Students who choose to study this major are likely to have many job opportunities after her graduation. Biomedical engineering is a hybrid science. They incorporate engineering principles with medicine and biology. Every year, biomedical engineers introduce new technologies to help people overcome her physical handicaps. Biomedical engineering has also evolved to meet the needs of people looking for alternative treatments—ones that are very different from what her doctors traditionally provided in the past. They say that this field of study is perfect for people who are as interested in medicine as they are in engineering and technology, as they can satisfy needs for both. These individuals are sure to thrive in this new and exciting field.

Feature 4: Unity

Unity in a paragraph means that all the sentences are related to the topic sentence and its controlling idea. Good writers stay on topic by making sure that each sentence fits clearly within the paragraph. In other words, each sentence in the paragraph should help to better explain and clarify the topic sentence.

ACTIVITY 11 | Analyzing a paragraph for unity

Read the problem-solution paragraph and answer the questions that follow.

> **WORDS TO KNOW** Paragraph 2.5
>
> **concentration:** (n) total attention to something
> **messy:** (adj) disorderly; not clean
> **productive:** (adj) getting good results
>
> **reduce:** (v) to make something smaller
> **tie up:** (v phr) to fasten together

PARAGRAPH 2.5

Organizing the Workspace

People who have trouble studying or working may benefit from cleaning up their **messy** workspace. A well-organized workspace will help increase **concentration** and work quality. In order to **reduce** clutter[1], unused items need to be thrown away. The fewer things on a person's desk, the better. This may be a good time to think about saving money and buying fewer office supplies. Adding a bookshelf can also help to organize a workspace. Bookshelves are beneficial because the objects in them are always visible. It is much easier to find something that is on a bookshelf than in a drawer. Finally, power cords and cables should be **tied up**. A clean and organized workspace is the key to being more **productive**.

[1]clutter: a mess

1. What is the purpose of this paragraph? Begin your sentence with *The purpose of ...*

_____

_____

2. Which sentence does not maintain the unity of this paragraph? Cross it out.

ACTIVITY 12 | Maintaining unity

Read the classification paragraph, which has problems with unity. Answer the questions that follow.

WORDS TO KNOW Paragraph 2.6

adapt: (v) to change, adjust
basically: (adv) for the most part
conflict: (n) a disagreement

fantasy: (n) the product of a creative imagination
plot: (n) the main story in a play or novel

PARAGRAPH 2.6

Movie Types

[1] There are many ways to classify movies, and one method is by general category—fiction, true story, and hybrid[1]. [2] Most movies fall into the category of fiction because the story for the film is not based on real events. [3] The characters and **plot** are not real, and the story can be drama, science fiction, or **fantasy**. [4] One such example is the *Batman* series, since everyone knows that Batman is not a real person. [5] I loved this type of movie when I was a child. [6] Another category is the true story. [7] This popular movie style tells the story of a real person—living or dead—or an event. [8] In fact, it is often **adapted** from the written account of a person or event. [9] One example that comes to mind is *Lincoln*, the film which details the last few months of U.S. President Abraham Lincoln's life. [10] Lincoln is one of the most beloved presidents of the United States. [11] Finally, there is the hybrid film, which is **basically** a combination of the two. [12] The word *hybrid* is also used to describe a type of car. [13] In this type of film, the writer takes a real event or person and adds fictional information, often to make the film more interesting. [14] One of the most famous examples of this type of film is *The Perfect Storm*. [15] In it, the director adds a fictional personal **conflict** between two of the men on the fishing boat that sank in 1991. [16] With these three types of film readily available to moviegoers, there is always something for everyone at the movie theater.

[1]hybrid: combining two types of things

1. What is the topic sentence of this paragraph?

_____

_____

2. There are three sentences that do not belong in this paragraph. Write the numbers of the sentences that do not belong. _____

Feature 5: Coherence

Writing has **coherence** when all of the ideas are organized and flow smoothly and logically from one to the next. When a paragraph is coherent, the reader can follow the ideas more easily.

Three important features of coherence are:

- logical order
- repetition of key words
- use of transitional words and phrases

ACTIVITY 13 | Using logical order

The following sentences form a paragraph, but they are not in the right order. Number the sentences in the correct order from 1 to 7. One of the sentences does not follow the unity of the paragraph. Cross it out.

_____ **a.** The other way is to join a sports team.

_____ **b.** It has exercise equipment, weights for lifting, and exercise classes to stay fit.

_____ **c.** Some students prefer to just do a lot of walking on campus.

_____ **d.** With a fitness club and team sports, college students have two good ways to stay in shape.

_____ **e.** There are two easy ways for college students to stay physically fit and active.

_____ **f.** Colleges have a variety of sports teams, including informal teams that do not compete with other colleges.

_____ **g.** All types of teams can be fun, and many students stay active this way.

_____ **h.** First, students can use the college fitness club.

Students learn yoga at a university in Shenyang, China.

ACTIVITY 14 | Repetition of key words

Look at the paragraph that you put in order in Activity 13, and answer the following questions.

1. What is the topic of the paragraph?

_____

2. What is the writer's purpose?

_____

_____

3. What key words does the writer repeat to keep the reader focused on the topic?

_____

_____

Transitional Words and Phrases

Transitional words and phrases are essential to maintain the flow and coherence of a paragraph. They are the links between ideas. Here are some common transitions. For more information on transitions and connectors, see the *Writer's Handbook*.

PURPOSE	EXAMPLES
To give examples	for example, for instance
To add information	and, also, in addition
To compare or contrast	in contrast, however, by comparison, on the other hand
To show time	finally, after that, before, next
To emphasize	obviously, in fact, clearly
To show sequence	first (second, third, etc.), next, at the same time
To show result	therefore, for these reasons, as a result
To summarize	in conclusion, in sum

ACTIVITY 15 | Using transitions

Read the following paragraph. Circle the correct transition word or phrase in parentheses.

Hiking the Sierra Madre Mountains

[1] (After / Before) exploring Mexico's Sierra Madre Mountains, adventurers should follow some important steps. [2] (After that / First), make sure you have comfortable hiking shoes. [3] (In fact / In addition), be sure to bring extra clothing because the temperature will decrease the higher you climb. It is especially important to bring enough water with you. Most experts recommend that hikers have at least two liters (8.5 cups) of water per day. [4] (In addition / For instance), it is a smart idea to bring a water filter so that you can safely drink from a natural source in case you run out. [5] (Finally / In conclusion), make sure you bring some food with you, such as protein bars or nuts, to give you the energy you need to finish the hike. Having an enjoyable and safe hiking trip in the Sierra Madre Mountains depends on these things.

A backpacker in Copper Canyon, Sierra Madre Mountains, Mexico

BUILDING BETTER VOCABULARY

WORDS TO KNOW

adapt (v) AW
alternative (n) AW
basically (adv)
concentration (n) AW
conflict (n) AW
decline (n) AW
device (n) AW
fantasy (n)

interfere (v)
major (adj) AW
messy (adj)
on average (phr)
permanent (adj)
plot (n)
poison (n)
productive (adj)

reduce (v)
release (n) AW
signal (v)
significantly (adv) AW
stimulate (v)
substance (n)
tie up (v phr)
unlike (prep)

ACTIVITY 16 | Word associations

Circle the word or phrase that is more closely related to the bold word or phrase on the left.

1. basically	simply	specifically
2. decline	increase	decrease
3. device	idea	thing
4. fantasy	real	unreal
5. messy	mixed up	separated
6. on average	normally	rarely
7. plot	character	story line
8. poison	dangerous	delicious
9. tie up	bring together	separate
10. unlike	better	different

ACTIVITY 17 | Collocations

Fill in the blank with the word that most naturally completes the phrase.

alternative	decline	major	reduce	significantly

1. a better _____

2. in order to _____ the number

3. a(n) _____ development

4. a(n) _____ in the population

5. _____ better than before

interfere	productive	release	signal	substance

6. _____ a change in the weather

7. a(n) _____ sales meeting

8. _____ with an investigation

9. a poisonous _____

10. the _____ of the prisoner

ACTIVITY 18 | Word forms

Complete each sentence with the correct word form. Use the correct form of the verbs.

NOUN	VERB	ADJECTIVE	ADVERB	SENTENCES
adaptation	adapt	adaptive / adaptable	adaptively	**1.** Some computerized exams are _____ ; that is, they produce different questions based on the answer to previous answers. **2.** It is difficult for some immigrants to _____ to a new culture.
concentration	concentrate	concentrated / concentrating		**3.** Without a certain amount of _____, it is almost impossible to do well on standardized tests. **4.** During our house remodel, we _____ on renovating the kitchen.

NOUN	VERB	ADJECTIVE	ADVERB	SENTENCES
conflict	conflict	conflicted / conflicting		**5.** There was a _____ of interest between the two companies. **6.** The witnesses gave _____ reports of what happened during the robbery.
permanence		permanent	permanently	**7.** That statue has been a _____ fixture on the college campus. **8.** Dr. Hadeed's family decided to _____ move to the country.
stimulation	stimulate	stimulated / stimulating		**9.** Psychiatrists sometimes use brain _____ to help their patients. **10.** The hope is that these taxes will _____ the economy.

ACTIVITY 19 | Vocabulary in writing

Choose five words from Words to Know. Write a complete sentence with each word.

1. _____

2. _____

3. _____

4. _____

5. _____

BUILDING BETTER SENTENCES

ACTIVITY 20 | Editing from teacher comments

Read the teacher's comments. Then on a separate piece of paper, revise the paragraph with corrections.

PARAGRAPH 2.8

Coffee vs. Tea

Coffee and tea are two of the most popular beverages in the world, but they are
wf
<u>vast</u> different. First of all, <u>tea more ancient than coffee</u>. *frag* It was discovered thousands

of years ago in Asia. Coffee, on the other hand, originated in <u>yemen and ethiopia</u> *cap*

in the ninth century. Another difference between the two drinks is their original
v form
form. Coffee is cultivated from a bean while tea <u>made</u> from tea leaves. This means

that the method of production also differs, with coffee being more difficult. Finally,
s/v agr
<u>researchers has found</u> some benefits to drinking coffee but also some harmful effects.

Tea, on the other hand, contains tannins, which may reduce the risk of cancer and

heart disease. Regardless of their possible effects, both of these drinks are enjoyed by
s/p
<u>million</u> of people every day.

Moacir Ribeiro da Silva sifts coffee beans at Nova Cintra's Farm in Espirito Santo do Pinhal, Brazil.

ACTIVITY 21 | Combining sentences

Combine the ideas into one sentence. You may change the word forms, but do not change or omit any ideas. There may be more than one answer. See Unit 1 for more information.

1. Children should learn behavior.
The behavior should be appropriate.
They do this in the classroom.

_____

_____

2. Using cell phones is disruptive.
Using cell phones is disrespectful.
People use cell phones during meetings.

_____

_____

3. A home can be damaged.
The damage can be permanent.
The damage is caused by hurricane-force winds.

_____

_____

ACTIVITY 22 | Writing sentences

Write an original sentence using the words listed.

1. (adapt / unlike) _____

_____

2. (messy / permanently) _____

_____

3. (conflict / major) _____

_____

4. (reduce / signal) _____

_____

5. (interfere / productive) _____

_____

WRITING

ACTIVITY 23 | Writing a paragraph

Follow these steps to write a paragraph.

1. Choose one of the additional topics for writing on the next page.

   Topic: _____

2. On a separate piece of paper, brainstorm ideas for about five minutes.

3. Use your brainstorming notes to choose a controlling idea. Write a topic sentence.

   Topic sentence: _____

   _____

4. Write your paragraph on a separate piece of paper. Follow these guidelines:

   • Include the three features of a well-written paragraph: It has a topic sentence.
     Every sentence relates to the topic. It has a concluding sentence.
   • Indent the first sentence of your paragraph.
   • Focus on clarity, unity, and coherence.
   • Use transitional words and phrases to add coherence.

If you need ideas for wording, see *Useful Words and Phrases* in the *Writer's Handbook.*

ACTIVITY 24 | Peer editing

Exchange paragraphs with a partner. Read your partner's paragraph. Then use Peer Editing Form 2 in the *Writer's Handbook* to help you comment on your partner's writing. Consider your partner's comments as you revise your paragraph.

Five Proofreading Strategies

Follow these suggestions to proofread your writing. After you proofread, make your revisions and then check your writing once more.

1. **Take a break from your work.** After you have finished writing, put your writing aside. The more time you take, the better your proofreading will be. A day is ideal, but even a break of 30 minutes helps.
2. **Read your writing aloud.** This will help you to read your work more carefully and slowly. Also, when you hear your sentences, you may catch more errors.
3. **Read your paper backward.** Start proofreading your writing by starting with the last sentence. Then read the second to last sentence, the third to last, and so on.
4. **Cover your work.** With another piece of paper, cover up everything except the line that you are reading. This method may help you to focus more closely on each line.

5. **Pretend that you are someone else.** Reading your work through the eyes of the reader will help you to identify phrases or sentences that might be unclear.

For more tips on editing your writing, see the *Writer's Handbook*.

ACTIVITY 25 | Proofreading your writing

Proofread your paragraph, using one or two of the strategies presented. Then revise your writing.

Additional Topics for Writing

Here are five ideas for writing a paragraph. Follow your teacher's instructions, and choose one or more topics to write about. Do not use the topic that you used in Activity 23.

TOPIC 1: Look at the photo at the beginning of this unit. Write a paragraph describing a traditional dance in your country.

TOPIC 2: Write a paragraph comparing life in high school and life in college.

TOPIC 3: Write a paragraph classifying the different types of shoes that are available and what each type is for.

TOPIC 4: Write about a typical problem for a high school student, and offer two suggestions to overcome this problem.

TOPIC 5: Write about the best way to make new friends.

TEST PREP

TIP

Before you begin writing, make sure that you understand the assignment. Underline key words in the writing prompt, and refer to them as you write. Second, follow the directions. Write on the assigned topic. Do not write more than is requested. If the assignment asks for a 150-word response, be sure that your written response comes close to that. Students do not get extra points for writing more than is required.

You should spend about 25 minutes on this task. Write about the following topic:

Compare the weather in two cities, regions, or countries that you know. How many seasons do they each have? How are their climates similar? How are they different?

Include any relevant supporting details from your background knowledge. Remember to include a topic sentence, supporting sentences, and a concluding sentence. Use descriptive language and clear pronoun reference. Write at least 150 words.

3 | Types of Paragraphs

OBJECTIVES
- Understand cause-effect, comparison, classification, and problem-solution paragraphs
- Recognize and edit for subject-verb agreement
- Use correct word forms in writing
- Write a paragraph with a clear purpose

Tourists viewing murals by Fernando Castro Pacheco in the Governor's Palace, Mérida, Mexico

FREEWRITE | Look at the photo and read the caption. Would you like to do this on your vacation? On a separate piece of paper, write about what you typically do on vacation.

ELEMENTS OF GREAT WRITING

Common Paragraph Types

In this unit, you will learn about four common types of paragraphs: cause-effect, comparison, classification, and problem-solution. Each type of paragraph differs in its purpose. As you study these four types of paragraphs, pay special attention to the characteristics, or features, of each.

Cause-Effect Paragraphs

A **cause-effect paragraph** answers the question "How did something happen?" or "What is the result?" of an action or event. It has the following features:

- explains the reason or reasons that something happened (focus-on-causes)
- lists the results or effects of an action or event (focus-on-effects)

If your topic is Internet addiction, you might decide to write a paragraph on the causes or reasons teens become addicted to the Internet. Alternatively, you might want to write a paragraph on the effects that Internet addiction has on teens.

ACTIVITY 1 | Analyzing a cause-effect paragraph

Read the paragraph and answer the questions that follow.

> **WORDS TO KNOW** Paragraph 3.1
>
> **abandoned:** (adj) left behind; empty
> **commercial:** (adj) related to business
> **consequence:** (n) the result of doing something
> **doubtful:** (adj) uncertain; questionable
> **shrink:** (v) to make or become smaller

PARAGRAPH 3.1

A Sea without Life

Since the 1960s, the Aral Sea in Central Asia has **shrunk** to less than 10 percent of its original size, which has led to many negative **consequences**. For one, the amount of salt in the water has increased, killing the fish and sea life that used to live in the sea. Unfortunately, this has destroyed the fishing industry, an important source of employment for local residents. The South Aral Sea used to be a busy **commercial** region, but the dry sea beds are now full of **abandoned** boats and ships. Uzbekistan and Kazakhstan have made some efforts to save this body of water, but it is **doubtful** that the South Aral Sea will ever return to its former size and beauty. Instead, the area will continue to suffer from the negative effects of losing this valuable sea.

**Abandoned ships in what was the
Aral Sea, Uzbekistan**

1. What is the purpose of this paragraph? Begin your sentence with *The purpose of* ...

   _____

   _____

2. Does this paragraph focus on the causes or the effects of the South Aral Sea problem?

   _____

3. What is the topic sentence?

   _____

   _____

4. What is the controlling idea in the topic sentence?

   _____

5. What specific details are used to support the controlling idea?

   _____

   _____

   _____

6. Is the concluding sentence a restatement, a suggestion, or a prediction?

   _____

ACTIVITY 2 | Developing ideas for a cause-effect paragraph

Complete the steps below to develop your ideas for a cause-effect paragraph.

1. Choose a topic from the list below, or think of your own topic.

- The effects of learning to speak a second language
- The causes of car accidents
- The effects of lying
- The effects of exercise
- The causes of stress

Your topic: _____

2. On a separate piece of paper, brainstorm ideas for your topic. Write down as many ideas as you can in five minutes.

3. Review your ideas and circle the best ones. Then fill in the information below.

a. Who is your audience? How much do they know about your topic?

_____

b. Will you focus on causes or effects?

_____

c. Purpose statement:

_____

_____

d. Topic sentence with a controlling idea:

_____

_____

e. Supporting details (list two to four):

_____

_____

_____

_____

Comparison Paragraphs

A **comparison paragraph** answers the question "How are two things the same or different?" or "What different elements exist in one thing?" A comparison paragraph does one of the following:

- compares similarities or differences between two things
- compares strengths and weaknesses of one thing
- compares advantages and disadvantages of one thing

ACTIVITY 3 | Analyzing a comparison paragraph

Read the paragraph and answer the questions that follow.

> **WORDS TO KNOW** Paragraph 3.2
>
> **be related to:** (v phr) to be connected to by family; to be associated with
> **fascinating:** (adj) very interesting
> **guarantee:** (v) to promise
>
> **integral:** (adj) necessary, essential
> **interaction:** (n) communication or direct involvement

PARAGRAPH 3.2

Friends vs. Family

Personal relationships are an **integral** part of human **interaction**, but relationships with friends are different from those with family. First of all, people choose friends based on common interests and personalities. They tend to share the same hobbies and get along well. Family relationships, however, are based on who you **are related to**. Being blood relatives does not **guarantee** an easy and close relationship. For instance, a grandfather may view the world in a much different way from a teenager. In fact, even the relationship between twins can be difficult. Another difference between friends and family is the length of the relationship. Relationships with friends can last a short time, or they can last for years. On the other hand, family relationships are forever. Relationships with friends and with family members are **fascinating** because of their differences.

Siblings playing chess in Abu Dhabi

1. What is the purpose of this paragraph? Begin your sentence with *The purpose of* ...

_____

_____

2. What is the controlling idea in the topic sentence?

_____

3. Check (✓) what this comparison paragraph does. Be prepared to explain your answers.

_____ **a.** discusses two subjects   _____ **c.** contrasts differences

_____ **b.** compares similarities   _____ **d.** shows advantages/disadvantages

ACTIVITY 4 | Developing ideas for a comparison paragraph

Complete the steps below to develop your ideas for a comparison paragraph.

1. Choose a topic from the list below, or think of your own topic.

- The similarities between two influential leaders
- The differences between swimming in a pool and swimming at the beach
- The differences between traveling 100 years ago and traveling today
- The advantages and disadvantages of using an e-book

Your topic: _____

2. On a separate piece of paper, brainstorm ideas for your topic. Write down as many ideas as you can in five minutes.

3. Review your ideas and circle the best ones. Then fill in the information below.

a. Purpose statement: _____

_____

b. Topic sentence with a controlling idea: _____

_____

_____

c. Supporting details (list two to four): _____

_____

_____

_____

Classification Paragraphs

A **classification paragraph** separates something into categories or groups. It has the following features:

- focuses on a specific topic (person, idea, etc.) that can be classified
- describes the different categories of that topic
- includes descriptions or identifying characteristics of each category

There is often more than one way to classify a group of items. In a classification paragraph, the controlling idea tells the basis of the writer's categorization. For example, cars could be categorized by price, use, or manufacturer. Movies could be categorized by type (genre), country of origin, or when they were made. When choosing the basis of classification, make sure that the categories are distinct and do not overlap.

ACTIVITY 5 | Analyzing a classification paragraph

Read the paragraph and answer the questions that follow.

> **WORDS TO KNOW** Paragraph 3.3
>
> **combination:** (n) a joining of different parts
> **distinct:** (adj) different from something else
> **endurance:** (n) the ability to suffer through difficulty
>
> **mentally:** (adv) in a manner related to the mind
> **motivated:** (adj) having a strong desire to do something

PARAGRAPH 3.3

Types of Runners

In the world of track-and-field, there are three different types of runners: sprinters, middle-distance runners, and distance runners. Sprinters run the shortest distances (for example, 100 meters), and the races may only last for 10 to 20 seconds. Sprinters generally have fast, explosive muscles, and their bodies are typically extremely muscular. The second type of runner, the middle-distance runner, runs longer races, such as the 800-meter (1/2-mile) run. A good middle-distance runner must have a **combination** of speed and **endurance**. The final type of runner is the distance runner. Physically speaking, a distance runner is quite **distinct** from a sprinter. He or she typically has a thin body and runs races that are anywhere from 1,600 to 10,000 meters (one to six miles) long. Because their races are longer and take more time to complete, distance runners need to be **mentally** strong so they can stay **motivated** over the length of a long race. Because of the different requirements, track-and-field runners differ according to the distances they run.

1. What is the purpose of this paragraph? Begin your sentence with *The purpose of ...*

   _____

   _____

2. What is the topic sentence?

   _____

3. How many types of runners are classified? _____

   List the types: _____

4. What two characteristics does the writer use to classify the runners?

   _____

   _____

   _____

5. Is the concluding sentence a restatement, suggestion, opinion, or prediction?

   _____

Grammar: Subject-Verb Agreement in the Simple Present

EXPLANATION	EXAMPLES
Use the *–s* form of the verb with third-person singular nouns and *he, she,* or *it.*	My **teacher gives** me helpful suggestions about my writing. **She makes** me a better writer.
Collective nouns are usually singular. Use the third-person singular form of the verb.	The **team wins** every game. The **couple works** in the city.
Plural nouns such as *people* or *children* use the third-person plural form of the verb.	**People** from many countries **visit** Shanghai.
Pronouns with *every-, some-,* or *any-* are always singular. Nouns with *each* or *every* are also singular.	**Everyone has** an accent of some kind. **Every** student **needs** a book and a workbook.
The verb should always agree with the subject of the sentence, not other nouns in the sentence.	A main **product** of Brazil and Colombia **is** coffee. **Animals** that eat meat **are** carnivorous.
One is followed by a singular verb. *All* or *some* can be followed by a singular or plural verb.	**One** of the bridges **is** closed. **All/Some** of the **students are** here. **All/Some** of the **information is** correct.
The noun after *there is* or *there are* is the subject of that sentence. Use *is* with a singular noun and *are* with a plural noun.	There **is** a **dictionary** on the table. There **are** three **reasons** for their decision.
Gerunds (*-ing* words used as nouns) are singular.	**Making** mistakes **is** an important part of learning.

ACTIVITY 6 | Correcting subject-verb agreement errors

Find the subject-verb agreement error in each sentence and correct it.

1. In my country, most people lives near the coast because the interior is too dry.

2. One of the basic principles of economics are that we have to make choices with our resources.

3. Sometimes parents and a child does not agree on what is best for the child's future.

4. People say that the airline industry is in trouble and airlines face many economic problems, but all of the flights out of the New York City area is usually full.

5. Many students are not prepared for the amount of studying they has to do in college.

6. There is several problems with that approach.

7. Playing sports such as soccer and basketball are very hard on an athlete's knees.

8. While many large animals are still endangered, some smaller species is doing better.

9. Anyone with a student ID card, including part-time students, are allowed to use the gym.

10. The family always vacation in Europe.

ACTIVITY 7 | Editing for subject-verb agreement

Read the classification paragraph and find the five errors in subject-verb agreement. Underline the errors and write the corrections above them.

> **WORDS TO KNOW** Paragraph 3.4
>
> **actual:** (adj) real; exact **display:** (n) a show

Celebrating with Fireworks

In many countries around the world, shooting fireworks into the sky are a traditional way to celebrate special occasions. Some countries use fireworks to mark their independence. For instance, Mexicans celebrates Independence Day on September 16th with parades, fairs, fireworks, and rodeos. Other countries have fireworks **displays** as part of an **actual** competition. On the last Saturday in July, the Sumidagawa Fireworks Festival is held in Japan. It is a 300-year-old contest to see which fireworks company have the most beautiful display. Perhaps the most common use of fireworks are seen on December 31st, when many countries celebrate the beginning of the new year at midnight. People across the world uses spectacular fireworks in a variety of ways.

Summer fireworks on the Sumida River in Tokyo, Japan

Grammar: Word Forms

When you are writing, be sure to use the correct form of a word (noun, verb, adjective, or adverb). One word may have several forms. For example, *move* is a verb, and *movement* is a noun. Note that not all words have all four forms. Here are some examples:

NOUN	VERB	ADJECTIVE	ADVERB
difference	differ	different	differently
quickness	quicken	quick	quickly
repetition	repeat	repetitive, repeated	repetitively, repeatedly
writing	write	written	Ø

ACTIVITY 8 | Editing for errors in word form

Read the classification paragraph and find the seven errors in word form. Underline each error and write the correct form above it.

WORDS TO KNOW Paragraph 3.5

adjustment: (n) a small change
engaged: (adj) interested in something

particularly: (adv) especially
strategy: (n) a plan to achieve a goal

PARAGRAPH 3.5

Academic Success

Most college students hope to achievement academic success, but sometimes they are not sure how to reach this goal. Of course, they know about the importance of note-taking skills and reviewing information before an exam. However, there are other **strategies** that can help. Juan Rodriguez discovered this in a **particularly** difficult calculus class. Choosing to sit in the front of the class was one of his strategies. When he sat there, he paid more attentive to the lecture and was more **engaged**. Another strategy was previewing the information that the instructor was going to introduction. Juan would go over the new material the day before the lecture and come to class with an idea of that day's lecture topic. He was more comfort with the information because it was not new to him. Finally, Juan found a classmate who was already good at calculus. By asking for his classmate's help, Juan received different explain from those of his instructor. Having this "expert" friend who explained difficult math ideas allowed Juan to process calculus more easy. If a student makes some **adjustments** to his or her academic habits, as Juan did, he or she will likely be more succeed.

ACTIVITY 9 | Developing ideas for a classification paragraph

Complete the steps below to develop your ideas for a classification paragraph.

1. Choose a topic from the list below, or think of your own topic.

   • Parenting styles
   • Types of airline jobs
   • Types of students on a campus
   • Types of inexpensive or free entertainment

   Your topic: _____

2. On a separate piece of paper, brainstorm ideas for your topic. Write down as many ideas as you can in five minutes.

3. Review your ideas and circle the best ones. Then fill in the information below.

   a. Purpose statement:

   _____

   _____

   b. Topic sentence with a controlling idea:

   _____

   _____

   c. Supporting details (list two to four):

   _____

   _____

   _____

Problem-Solution Paragraphs

A **problem-solution paragraph** focuses on an interesting problem. It has the following features:

- usually focuses on a current problem
- presents the problem in the topic sentence
- offers one or more solutions to the problem
- includes a final thought on the problem or solution

ACTIVITY 10 | Analyzing a problem-solution paragraph

Read the paragraph and answer the questions that follow.

> **WORDS TO KNOW** Paragraph 3.6
>
> **additional:** (adj) added; other   **impact:** (n) an effect
> **dilemma:** (n) a difficult choice

PARAGRAPH 3.6

The E-Book Solution

    While ordinary textbooks are certainly valuable and important, their production has a negative **impact** on the environment. Millions of trees are cut down each year to produce textbooks. One solution to this environmental **dilemma** is e-books. Since paper is not used in the production of e-books, trees are not destroyed for them. Using e-books rather than printed books also saves on old textbooks in landfills[1]. About one-quarter of all the trash in landfills is paper. The printing process has an **additional** impact on our water resources because making paper requires significant amounts of water. With the e-book technology that is available today, cutting down millions of trees to produce paper for traditional textbooks could become a thing of the past.

[1]landfill: a low-lying area filled in, often with garbage

1. What is the purpose of this paragraph? Begin your sentence with *The purpose of ...*

   _____

   _____

2. What problem is stated in the topic sentence?

   _____

3. What solution or solutions are presented?

   _____

4. What points support the solution(s)?

   _____

   _____

ACTIVITY 11 | Developing ideas for a problem-solution paragraph

Complete the steps below to develop your ideas for a problem-solution paragraph.

1. Choose a topic from the list below, or think of your own topic. If you choose your own topic, you might focus on a real problem that you would like to solve.

   • Children and electronic devices
   • Living within a financial budget
   • Cheating on exams
   • Inadequate public transportation

   Your topic: _____

2. On a separate piece of paper, brainstorm ideas for your topic. Write down as many ideas as you can in five minutes.

3. Review your ideas and circle the best ones. Then fill in the information below.

   a. Purpose statement: _____

   _____

   b. Topic sentence with a controlling idea: _____

   _____

   _____

   c. Supporting details (list two to four): _____

   _____

   _____

   _____

BUILDING BETTER VOCABULARY

WORDS TO KNOW

abandoned (adj) `AW`
actual (adj)
additional (adj)
adjustment (n) `AW`
be related to (v phr)
combination (n)
commercial (adj)
consequence (n) `AW`

dilemma (n) `AW`
display (n) `AW`
distinct (adj) `AW`
doubtful (adj)
endurance (n)
engaged (adj)
fascinating (adj)
guarantee (v) `AW`

impact (n) `AW`
integral (adj) `AW`
interaction (n) `AW`
mentally (adv) `AW`
motivated (adj) `AW`
particularly (adv)
shrink (v)
strategy (n) `AW`

ACTIVITY 12 | Word associations

Circle the word or phrase that is more closely related to the bold word or phrase on the left.

1. actual	real	fake
2. be related to	be associated with	be against
3. combination	individual	mixture
4. dilemma	difficult choice	good opportunity
5. fascinating	interesting	boring
6. impact	cause	effect
7. integral	necessary	unnecessary
8. interaction	disagreement	communication
9. particularly	generally	especially
10. shrink	improve	get smaller

ACTIVITY 13 | Collocations

Fill in the blank with the word or phrase that most naturally completes the phrase.

abandoned	commercial	doubtful	endurance	guarantee

1. it is _____ that

2. a busy _____ region

3. a money-back _____

4. a sport of _____

5. a(n) _____ house

consequences	display	distinct	motivated	strong

6. highly _____ to succeed

7. an amazing _____

8. mentally _____

9. quite _____ from each other

10. negative _____

Suffixes

Some words have **suffixes** or endings that indicate the part of speech. Notice the suffixes for these parts of speech:

PART OF SPEECH	COMMON SUFFIXES		EXAMPLES
Noun	-ion -ment -er -ness -ity / -ty -ence -ance	vacat<u>ion</u> entertain<u>ment</u> teach<u>er</u> sad<u>ness</u> activ<u>ity</u> differ<u>ence</u> domin<u>ance</u>	In this photo, you can see the **beauty** of a sunset. The **brightness** of the colorful clouds is striking. Moving to a new city is an **adjustment**.
Verb	-ify -ize -en -ate	class<u>ify</u> real<u>ize</u> short<u>en</u> gener<u>ate</u>	The city will **beautify** several neighborhoods. The neighborhoods will **organize** several work days.
Adjective	-ful -ent -able -ive -ial -y	beauti<u>ful</u> differ<u>ent</u> comfort<u>able</u> invent<u>ive</u> financ<u>ial</u> wind<u>y</u>	That is the most **beautiful** baby I have ever seen. Her hair is long and **curly**. The office is in an **industrial** zone.
Adverb	-ly	quick<u>ly</u>	Jasmine sings **beautifully**. She performs very **confidently**.

Sometimes a word can function as a different part of speech without the addition of a suffix. For example, the word *paint* can be a noun (*Where is the paint?*) or a verb (*Let's paint the kitchen.*). The word *hard* can be an adjective (*The candy is hard.*) or an adverb (*She studied hard.*). Always check your writing for the correct word forms.

ACTIVITY 14 | Identifying word forms

Study the word forms below and fill in the missing forms. If necessary, use a dictionary.

	NOUN	VERB	ADJECTIVE	ADVERB
1.	abandonment	abandon		Ø
2.		Ø	consequential	consequentially
3.	destruction			destructively
4.		Ø	regional	
5.		fascinate		Ø
6.	doubt			doubtfully
7.			residential	Ø

ACTIVITY 15 | Word forms

Complete each sentence with the correct word form. Use the correct form of the verbs.

NOUN	VERB	ADJECTIVE	ADVERB	SENTENCES
addition	add	additional	additionally	**1.** Our company is opening an _____ office in Tokyo. **2.** We expect to _____ three more offices next year.
endurance	endure	enduring		**3.** Runners need both _____ and strength to run a marathon. **4.** Servers in restaurants often have to _____ rude customers.
interaction	interact	interactive	interactively	**5.** Online learning is often _____. **6.** The _____ with sales staff is one reason customers like to shop in stores.
motivation	motivate	motivated / motivational		**7.** Should colleges _____ their students to vote? **8.** Companies look for _____ employees.
strategy	strategize	strategic	strategically	**9.** The restaurant _____ placed its sign near the busy street. **10.** In June, Ana will _____ her next career move.

ACTIVITY 16 | Vocabulary in writing

Choose five words from Words to Know. Write a complete sentence with each word.

1. _____

2. _____

3. _____

4. _____

5. _____

BUILDING BETTER SENTENCES

ACTIVITY 17 | Error correction

This paragraph has five errors: subject-verb agreement (2), fragment (1), word form (1), and word order (1). Find and correct the errors.

PARAGRAPH 3.7

Olympics vs. Paralympics

Every four years, the best athletes around the world competes in the Olympics or the Paralympics. Although both competitions feature many of the same events and the highest level of performance. They are distinct programs. The most important different is between the athletes themselves. While Olympic athletes are able-bodied, Paralympians have some form of disability. They may been have born with physical problems, or they might have experienced injuries. This often means the athletes need special facilities. Another difference between the two are financial support. The Olympic Games and its athletes get much more money and more attention. Both sets of athletes demonstrate strength, speed, and endurance, so the Paralympians should get the same support.

American Oksana Masters competing in the women's cross-country skiing 5km sitting event at the 2018 Winter Paralympic Games in Pyeongchang, South Korea

ACTIVITY 18 | Scrambled sentences

Unscramble the words and phrases to write complete sentences.

1. a better exercise / over 50 / than / for people / running / swimming is

_____

_____

2. solution / can be / for / services / busy / grocery delivery / a / families / convenient

_____

_____

3. your sleep / common / a / impact / on / several / can have / activities / negative

_____

_____

4. by people / driverless cars / over cars / have / several / distinct advantages / driven

_____

_____

5. apartments / on-campus housing: / of / two choices / or dorms / have / students

_____

_____

ACTIVITY 19 | Combining sentences

Combine the ideas into one sentence. You may change the word forms, but do not change or omit any ideas. There may be more than one answer.

1. Oksana Masters was born in Ukraine in 1989.

She had severe physical problems.

Now she is an outstanding American athlete.

She competes in cross-country skiing and cycling.

_____

_____

2. Alligators have U-shaped faces.

Their faces are wide and short.

Crocodiles have slender faces.

They are almost V-shaped.

_____

_____

3. Researchers plan to design a wind turbine.

It will be taller than the Eiffel Tower.

It will have 650-foot (198-meter) blades.

It could reduce the cost of wind power by 50 percent.

_____

_____

Wind turbines in Oiz eolic park, Spain

WRITING

ACTIVITY 20 | Writing your own paragraph

Follow these steps.

1. Choose a type of paragraph from this unit that you would like to write: cause-effect, comparison, classification, or problem-solution.

   Type of paragraph: _____

   Your topic: _____

2. On a separate piece of paper, brainstorm ideas for your topic. Write down as many ideas as you can in five minutes.

3. Review your ideas and circle the best ones. Then fill in the information below.

   a. Purpose statement:

   _____

   _____

   b. Topic sentence with a controlling idea:

   _____

   _____

   c. Supporting details (list two to four):

   _____

   _____

   _____

   _____

   d. Conclusion:

   _____

   _____

4. On a separate piece of paper, write your paragraph.

Editing

After you write, it is important to edit (revise) your work. When you do this, look for ways to better explain your ideas, add stronger support, and use words that more accurately express what you want to say. Sharing your writing with a peer and receiving comments from him or her is a good way to get ideas for how to improve your work.

ACTIVITY 21 | Peer editing

Exchange papers with a partner. Read your partner's paragraph. Then use Peer Editing Form 3 in the *Writer's Handbook* to help you comment on your partner's writing. Consider your partner's comments as you revise your paragraph.

> **WRITER'S NOTE** Proofreading Your Work
>
> Experienced writers know that it takes more than just one session of writing to create a well-written paragraph. Proofreading is an essential last step in the editing process. Try to proofread your work at least twice and make any necessary changes to it before turning it in to your instructor.

ACTIVITY 22 | Proofreading your work

Use the following checklist to review your final draft. Use all the feedback that you have received, including peer feedback, instructor comments, and self-evaluation. In addition, try reading your paragraph aloud. When you finish, add a title to your paragraph.

- ☐ The ideas in my paragraph will be interesting to readers.
- ☐ The topic sentence makes the purpose of my paragraph clear: to classify, compare, explain causes and/or effects, or present a problem and solution.
- ☐ Details in the body clearly support the topic sentence.
- ☐ The concluding sentence brings the paragraph to a logical end.
- ☐ I used correct subject-verb agreement in each sentence.
- ☐ I used correct word forms.

Additional Topics for Writing

Here are five ideas for writing a paragraph. Choose a topic and follow your teacher's instructions.

TOPIC 1: Look at the photo at the beginning of this unit. Write a paragraph comparing the Governor's Palace in Mérida, Mexico, to a government building in your country.

TOPIC 2: Write a paragraph comparing two types of music.

TOPIC 3: Describe a problem in your community, and propose one or more solutions.

TOPIC 4: What are the causes and/or effects of dropping out of school?

TOPIC 5: Classify different ways students spend their summer vacations.

TEST PREP

> **TIP**
>
> Leave time to check your writing for these issues before you finish:
>
> - Replace any contractions with full forms. Contractions are not used in academic writing.
> - Check that you used proper word forms and spelled verbs correctly.
> - Avoid general terms such as *great, nice,* and *big*. Use specific, descriptive words.

You should spend about 25 minutes on this task. Write a paragraph about the following topic:

Compare today's mobile phones with those of five or ten years ago.

Make sure you have identified your main points of comparison before you begin writing. Include details and examples from your knowledge or experience. Write at least 150 words.

A man uses a smartphone to live stream news.

4 | Classification Essays: Moving from Paragraph to Essay

OBJECTIVES
- Understand similarities between paragraphs and essays
- Use subject adjective clauses
- Brainstorm with a cluster diagram
- Write a classification essay

Thousands of natural redheads from around the world gather each year for the Redhead Days Festival in Breda, Netherlands.

FREEWRITE | Look at the photo and read the caption. Besides hair color, what are other ways that people classify themselves? On a separate piece of paper, write about different ways you classify yourself or others.

ELEMENTS OF GREAT WRITING

Comparing Paragraphs and Essays

In Units 1–3, we reviewed the basics of paragraph writing. We learned that a paragraph is a group of sentences about one idea that includes a main topic and a controlling idea.

An **essay** is similar to a paragraph in its organization and order, but an essay includes more information about a topic. In an essay, each main point is presented in an individual body paragraph. The paragraph supports the point with examples, explanations, and details.

Notice the relationship between the parts of a paragraph and the parts of an essay.

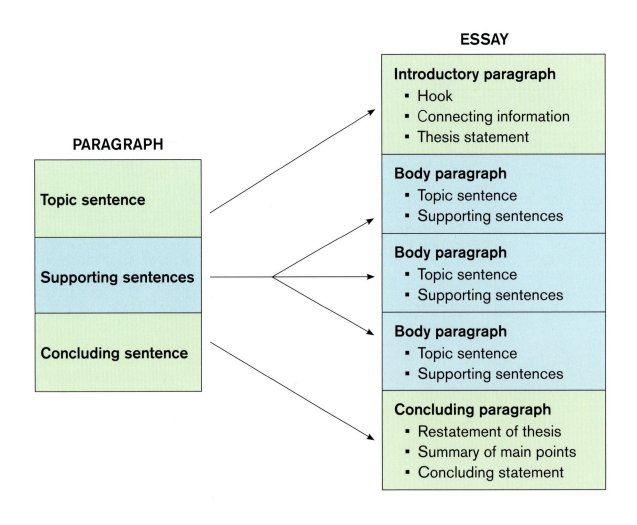

Read the paragraph and answer the questions that follow.

> **WORDS TO KNOW** Paragraph 4.1
>
> **classify:** (v) to put in groups with similar characteristics
>
> **form:** (n) type; kind

PARAGRAPH 4.1

The Many Faces of Acting

Modern acting comes in a variety of **forms** and can be **classified** into three types: stage acting, television acting, and film acting. Stage acting, which is the oldest form of acting, occurs in front of a live audience, in places ranging from large performance halls to small theaters. The next and probably the most well-known category of acting is television acting. This type of acting is for weekly programs that are produced in a TV studio. The third and final type of acting is film acting for a movie. Film acting is similar to TV acting, but the process is more complex, and it takes longer to make a movie. Regardless of the type of acting, audience members appreciate actors for the many hours of enjoyment they provide.

1. What three forms of acting are discussed?

_____

_____

2. How could you expand this paragraph into an essay? What information could you add?

_____

_____

_____

3. How many body paragraphs would there probably be in the essay? What would the topic of each one be?

_____

_____

_____

_____

The Introductory Paragraph in an Essay

In an essay, the introductory paragraph starts with a hook, followed by connecting information, which leads to the thesis statement.

The Hook

A hook is found on the end of a fishing line and is used to catch fish. In writing, a **hook** is a sentence (or sentences) that catches the reader's attention at the beginning of the essay. Good writers use a hook to get the reader interested in the first paragraph of an essay. The hook gives the reader a reason to keep reading. Hooks can be questions, quotes, descriptions, or other interesting pieces of information that attract the reader.

Connecting Information

After the hook, the writer usually gives several sentences with **connecting information**, leading from the hook to the topic. These sentences logically lead to the thesis.

The Thesis Statement

The key sentence in a paragraph is called a topic sentence. In an essay, the key sentence is in the introductory paragraph and is called the **thesis statement**. The thesis statement gives the reader a clear idea of how the essay will be developed. The thesis statement may also include the **points of development**, or the main ideas that will be developed in the supporting paragraphs. It is often, but not always, the last sentence in the introduction. Sometimes the main idea or thesis may be found in two sentences.

Study the following introductory paragraph.

On hearing the word *vacation*, most people react positively. It can be a weekend trip, a last-minute getaway, or a trip around the world. Prospective travelers spend days, if not weeks, researching their travel destination. While the destination has a lot to do with the success of a trip, there are other factors to consider. Experienced travelers will argue that more important than where they go on vacation is who they go with. Vacations can be classified on the basis of who vacationers choose to travel with: with family, with friends, or alone.

Hook

Connecting information

Thesis statement with points of development

ACTIVITY 2 | Analyzing an essay

Read the essay based on Paragraph 4.1 and answer the questions that follow.

WORDS TO KNOW Essay 4.1

crucial: (adj) extremely important
entertaining: (adj) interesting and enjoyable
generation: (n) a group of people of approximately the same age
household: (n) home
practically: (adv) nearly, almost
range from: (v phr) to extend from; to cover

rehearse: (v) to practice, prepare for a performance
replacement: (n) a person or thing that takes the place of another
unique: (adj) one of a kind
visual: (adj) able to be seen
whichever: (adj) one or the other; no matter what

ESSAY 4.1

The Many Faces of Acting

1   Did you know that as recently as a few **generations** ago, one of the most common forms of entertainment was listening to actors in radio dramas? During the 1930s, for example, radio audiences had to imagine the scenery, the action, and even the physical appearance of the performers. Nowadays, it is difficult to imagine acting as a form of entertainment without a **visual** format. Modern acting comes in a variety of forms and can be classified into three types: stage acting, television acting, and film acting.

Actors and technicians work on the film *Robin Hood: Origins* in Dubrovnik, Croatia.

2   Of the modern types of acting, the oldest form is stage acting. Plays, **ranging from** Shakespearean classics to more modern hits, are performed in large theaters and on small community stages. In stage acting, the same performance is repeated, and the stage sets[1] stay the same for each performance. Rehearsing for stage acting can take months because all the actors must memorize their lines. In addition, stage acting is "live," so the use of understudies—or **replacement** actors—is **crucial**. A star who is injured or cannot perform is replaced by an understudy. Because there is no way to edit the performance as you would edit a film, stage performances can be excellent one day and uneven the next. Many people say that there is nothing more **entertaining** than watching actors performing live on the stage.

3   Perhaps the best-known type of acting is television acting. This type of acting generally is done for television programs produced in a studio. The story lines change from week to week as writers create new dialogs and scenes for the main characters. Actors come to work five days a week to **rehearse** their lines. On the final day, the TV cameras are turned on and filming begins. TV actors have the help of teleprompters[2] and advice from off-camera directors who can help them to deliver their lines. Television scenes can be filmed repeatedly until the actors get it right. With TVs in **practically** every **household**, it is no wonder this is the most familiar form of acting.

4   Finally, there is film acting. Film acting begins with a screenplay, which includes all the written information about the set and the actors' dialogs, and grows into a movie. It can be filmed anywhere in the world. For instance, if the story happens to take place in Brazil, the film crew and actors go on location in that country to film. While screenplays have a beginning, a middle, and an end, the filming of movies does not have to be in chronological[3] order. That is, actors may have to film the ending of the movie before working on scenes from the beginning. Because it is not a live performance, directors may request that an actor repeat a scene until they are happy with the results, which can mean a lot of work for the actors. For these reasons, film actors must be hard workers and have a lot of flexibility in how, and where, they work.

5   **Whichever** form it takes—stage, television, or film—acting as a form of entertainment ranks very high on most people's lists of favorite activities to watch. Still, it is interesting to note that different forms of acting have **unique** characteristics. Regardless of the type of acting one prefers, it is safe to say that audience members will continue to appreciate the craft of acting as long as it provides such enjoyable entertainment.

[1]set: place where an acting performance is given
[2]teleprompter: a machine that shows words for a speaker to read
[3]chronological: in time order

1. Find the hook. Is it a question, quote, description, or other interesting piece of information?

   _____

2. What connecting information is given between the hook and the thesis statement?

   _____

   _____

3. Underline the thesis statement. What points of development are given in the thesis?

   _____

4. Look back at the topic sentence of Paragraph 4.1, "The Many Faces of Acting." Find the sentence in Essay 4.1 that is similar to it. What is the purpose of this sentence in the essay?

   _____

   _____

5. What is an interesting point that the writer makes?

   _____

   _____

Classification Essays

A **classification essay** organizes or sorts things into categories. With any topic, the key is to select one **principle of organization**. The principle of organization is the method by which the writer analyzes the information in the essay. For example, in classifying types of movies, a writer can choose among several principles of organization: genre or film type, period in which the movie was made, audience type, character roles, etc.

ACTIVITY 3 | Completing the outline of a classification essay

Read the outline for Essay 4.1 to understand the essay's organization. Use the phrases below to complete the outline.

A lot of work for actors	Sets stay the same
Begins with a screenplay	Stories change every week
Best-known type of acting	Teleprompters give lines
Introduction	Television acting
Must memorize lines	Thesis statement
No editing	Type 3
Range from old plays to new ones	

Title: The Many Faces of Acting

I. _____

    A. Hook

    B. Connecting information

    C. _____

II. Body Paragraph 1 (Type 1): Stage acting

    A. General information

        1. Oldest type of acting

        2. _____

        3. Performed on large and small stages

    B. Performance/set

        1. Performance is repeated each night

        2. _____

    C. Actors' responsibilities

        1. Rehearse for months

        2. _____

        3. Importance of understudies

    D. Disadvantages

        1. _____

        2. Great one day/uneven the next

SUPPORT

III. Body Paragraph 2 (Type 2): _____

    A. General information

        1. _____

        2. TV programs

        3. Filmed in a studio

    B. Story

        1. _____

        2. Writers create new dialogs and scenes

    C. Actors' responsibilities

        1. Actors rehearse five days per week

        2. Filming on the last day

    D. Advantages

        1. _____

        2. Director's help

        3. Filmed until it is just right

IV. Body Paragraph 3 (_____): Film acting

    A. Process

        1. _____

        2. Becomes a movie

    B. Filming

        1. Filmed on location

        2. Scenes can be filmed in any order

    C. Advantages/disadvantages

        1. Repeat scenes until good results

        2. _____

    D. Actors' responsibilities

        1. Be a hard worker

        2. Be flexible in how and where they work

V. Conclusion

    A. Restate the thesis statement

    B. Summarize the main points

    C. Concluding statement: a prediction

SUPPORT

SUPPORT

Grammar: Subject Adjective Clauses

An **adjective clause** adds information about a noun or pronoun. It follows the noun, noun phrase, or pronoun it describes. **Subject adjective clauses** begin with a relative pronoun (*that*, *which*, or *who*) followed by a verb.

EXPLANATION	EXAMPLES
Use *that* or *which* for things. (*That* is more common.)	adjective clause Gumbo is a thick <u>soup</u> <u>that</u> <u>contains</u> seafood or meat. noun subj v
Use *who* or *that* for people. (*Who* is preferred.)	adjective clause A goalie is a <u>player</u> <u>who</u> <u>protects</u> his team's goal. noun subj v
No commas are used if the information in the adjective clause is necessary to clarify *who* or *what*.	A car <u>that has a large trunk</u> is a good choice for necessary information a family.
Use a comma(s) to separate the adjective clause if the information is not necessary to understand *who* or *what*.	A Hyundai Sonata, <u>which has a large trunk</u>, is a good unnecessary information choice for a family.

ACTIVITY 4 | Identifying subject adjective clauses

Underline the adjective clause in each of the following sentences.

1. Actors who perform in stage plays must be able to memorize all their lines.

2. African elephants, which have larger ears, are bigger than Asian elephants.

3. Movie theaters that offer reserved seats and full menus are becoming increasingly popular.

4. Ladders, which can be used to paint a house, can be surprisingly dangerous.

5. Saltwater aquariums, which can hold sharks, require a lot of maintenance.

ACTIVITY 5 | Writing subject adjective clauses

Combine the sentences, making the second sentence an adjective clause. Punctuate as needed.

1. Emma Watson knew she wanted to act at the age of six. She has appeared in all eight *Harry Potter* movies.

_____

_____

2. Movies often make a lot of money. These movies feature superheroes.

_____

_____

3. George W. Bush has taken up painting. He was the 43rd President of the United States.

_____

_____

4. Teachers can reschedule exams for students. These students have a good excuse.

_____

_____

5. Nowadays, many people use phone apps. These phone apps provide directions and traffic information.

_____

_____

6. Shakespeare wrote many plays. His plays were either tragic, humorous, or historical.

_____

_____

ACTIVITY 6 | Analyzing a classification essay

Read the essay and answer the questions that follow.

> **WORDS TO KNOW** Essay 4.2
>
> **basis:** (n) the main reason for something
> **face:** (v) to meet; to experience; to deal with
> **factor:** (n) a fact to be considered; a cause
> **flexible:** (adj) able to change easily
> **negotiate:** (v) to discuss in order to reach an agreement, bargain
> **personality:** (n) the total effect of a person's qualities
>
> **potential:** (adj) possible
> **prospective:** (adj) expected to be
> **react:** (v) to respond
> **skip:** (v) to miss, not do
> **solo:** (adj) by oneself, alone

ESSAY 4.2

Vacations for Everyone

1   On hearing the word _vacation_, most people **react** positively. It can be a weekend trip, a last-minute getaway, or a trip around the world. **Prospective** travelers spend days, if not weeks, researching their travel destination. While the destination has a lot to do with the success of a trip, there are other **factors** to consider. Experienced travelers will argue that more important than where they go on vacation is who they go with. Vacations can be classified on the **basis** of who vacationers choose to travel with: with family, with friends, or alone.

Vacationers enjoying a zipline over the Niagara River with a great view of Niagara Falls

2   Family travel is special and creates lasting memories, but it can also have some challenges. For one, the success of a trip often depends on the relationships that the family members have with one another. If two brothers do not get along at home, the chances are that they will fight during a vacation. Another **potential** problem of family travel is transportation. If a family is traveling by air, purchasing plane tickets for everyone can be very expensive. In addition, finding common places of interest is more complicated with family groups. For instance, a father might want to see the alligator farm while a mother wants to visit a museum and the kids scream for a trip to an amusement park. Regardless of the challenges families **may face** when traveling, this type of vacation always creates special memories.

3   Traveling with friends can be an unforgettable experience for several reasons. Close friends often have similar **personalities**, so they generally get along with each other and fight less than family members might on a trip. If differences over which sights to see do come up, good friends can often **negotiate** those differences rather quickly. Because each person covers only his or her individual expenses, costs tend not to be an issue. Furthermore, if friends are close, even a terrible trip will not ruin the friendship. In fact, friendships are often strengthened when friends share both good and bad travel memories. However, if friends do not know each other well or have not traveled together before, vacationing together may do more harm than good. All in all, traveling with friends can be a positive experience that results in a great vacation and, likely, a stronger friendship.

4   Finally, people can choose to travel alone. It takes a special person to attempt this type of travel as most travelers enjoy having company, but there can be some surprising benefits. For instance, **solo** travelers can be more **flexible** with transportation than those traveling in a large group. They can change plans more easily and have better chances of getting a seat on buses or planes since they only need one. Sightseeing and scheduling are also not a problem for solo travelers. They can choose to wake up late in the day, sightsee at night, or **skip** lunch if they feel like it. In addition, solo travelers are more likely to meet locals or other vacationers because they are more likely to want to talk with others. On the other hand, solo travelers might experience loneliness from not being able to share the amazing experiences they are having with someone. In spite of this, many solo travelers love the adventure and say that they learn a lot about themselves while traveling alone.

5   Different forms of travel are available to everyone. People who are comfortable with relatives enjoy family vacations. People who want to be sure to have the best time possible while avoiding arguments may travel with their closest friends. People who are comfortable alone and love the excitement of seeing new places may choose to travel alone. Whatever the personal preference, there is a travel choice for everyone.

1. What is the purpose of this essay? Begin your sentence with *The purpose ...*

_____

_____

2. Underline the thesis statement. What three points of development are given in the thesis statement?

_____

_____

3. Underline the topic sentences in the three body paragraphs in this essay.

4. Underline the concluding sentences in the three body paragraphs.

5. What is an interesting point that the writer included?

_____

_____

The Five-Paragraph Essay

An **essay** is a collection of paragraphs, organized much like an individual paragraph with an introduction, a body, and a conclusion. An essay can have as few as three paragraphs or as many as 10 (or more) paragraphs.

In this book, you will study the five-paragraph essay, a good model for writing all kinds of essays. In some classes, you may have to write a much longer essay, but the basic organization of a five-paragraph essay can easily be expanded for any kind of essay.

A five-paragraph essay consists of the following parts:

1. Introductory paragraph
2. First body paragraph
3. Second body paragraph
4. Third body paragraph
5. Concluding paragraph

ACTIVITY 7 | Analyzing an essay

Answer the following questions about Essay 4.2.

1. In the first body paragraph, what are some of the supporting details?

2. In the second body paragraph, what are some of the supporting details?

3. What are the advantages and disadvantages listed in body paragraph 3?

4. Is there any place where you would like more explanation or detail? If so, where?

5. Does the conclusion of the essay end with a suggestion, an opinion, or a prediction?

Understanding the Writing Process

No writer—not even a professional writer—sits down and writes an essay from the introduction to the conclusion. Effective writers approach an essay as many small pieces of writing that are done step by step. Here are seven steps that many writers follow when they write.

Step 1: Choose a topic. You can choose a topic in a couple of ways.

  a. Choose something familiar. It is easier to write about something you know well. It is even better to write about something you care or are excited about.

  b. Choose something that you are interested in and want to learn about. For example, if you have an interest in skydiving but have never tried it, you might decide to write about it.

Step 2: Brainstorm ideas for your topic. Here are three techniques you can try.

  a. **List ideas.** Write down everything about the topic that comes to mind. Do not worry about grammar, spelling, order, or organization. Just list ideas as fast as they come to you.

  b. **Make a cluster diagram.** Write down an idea and draw a circle around it. Branching off from that idea, draw lines to related ideas. For an essay about types of sports, a cluster diagram might look like this.

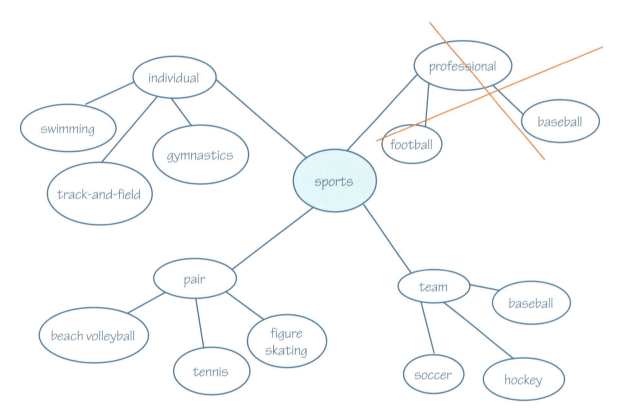

  c. **Freewrite.** Freewriting is a technique in which a writer writes whatever comes to his or her mind. The idea is to keep writing without stopping. Set a time limit and write continuously until that time has passed. This is a good technique to use when you are having trouble coming up with ideas.

Step 3: Select a purpose and outline. It is important to be clear on the purpose of the essay. Are you going to classify something? Compare two things? Show cause and effect? Present a problem and solution? Look at your brainstorming notes and circle the ideas that would fit your purpose. It is also helpful to create a purpose statement and refer to it as you write.

After deciding on the purpose of your essay, it is time to organize your ideas in a simple outline. Circle the best ideas in your brainstorming notes. Then group those ideas into three main categories. These will be the three points of development for your three body paragraphs.

There are several ways to write an outline, but many writers use this traditional format:

    I. Introduction

    II. Body

    III. Body

    IV. Body

    V. Conclusion

Step 4: Write the first draft. No two writers approach a writing assignment the same way. Some writers begin with the introduction and proceed from paragraph to paragraph. Other writers prefer to work on various paragraphs at different times. In fact, you do not need to start with the introductory paragraph. Some writers find it best to write a first draft of the introductory paragraph after they have completed the whole essay. Choose the order that works best for you.

Step 5: Get feedback. One of the best ways to improve your writing is to have someone else review it and offer suggestions. Review the explanation of Peer Editing in Unit 1, page 30.

Step 6: Reread, rethink, rewrite. Because it is hard to write a perfect paper on the first try, it is important to edit and make changes to improve the essay. As you revise your first draft, incorporate feedback from others and add any new ideas that you have to improve the essay.

Step 7: Proofread the final draft. Proofreading your final draft is an important final step in the writing process. Review the Five Proofreading Strategies in Unit 2, pages 56–57.

ACTIVITY 8 | Brainstorming with a cluster diagram

Choose one of the topics below or write your own. On a separate piece of paper, make a cluster diagram. Use the example in Step 2 as a model and add as many ideas as you can.

- Types of free entertainment
- Types of universities

- Types of shoppers
- Types of _____

Bikers wear face masks to protect themselves against pollution in Hanoi, Vietnam.

ACTIVITY 9 | Identifying a purpose

Read the following topics for a classification essay. Work with a partner to discuss the purpose and possible points of development for each. For item 4, use information from your cluster diagram in Activity 8.

1. Title: Types of Pollution

   Purpose: _The purpose of this essay is to describe three types of pollution and ways to reduce each._

   Three points of development: _fossil fuel emissions, animal farming, landfills/waste_

2. Title: Types of Food

   Purpose: _____

   Three points of development: _____

3. Title: Airplane Passengers

   Purpose: _____

   Three points of development: _____

4. Title: _____

   Purpose: _____

   Three points of development: _____

BUILDING BETTER VOCABULARY

WORDS TO KNOW

basis (n)	generation (n) AW	react (v) AW
classify (v) AW	household (n)	rehearse (v)
crucial (adj) AW	negotiate (v)	replacement (n) AW
entertaining (adj)	personality (n)	skip (v) AW
face (v)	potential (adj) AW	solo (adj)
factor (n) AW	practically (adv)	unique (adj) AW
flexible (adj) AW	prospective (adj) AW	visual (adj) AW
form (n)	range from (v phr) AW	whichever (adj) AW

ACTIVITY 10 | Word associations

Circle the word that is more closely related to the bold word on the left.

1. classify	teach	group
2. crucial	unimportant	essential
3. factor	cause	truth
4. form	type	subject
5. negotiate	disagree	bargain
6. potential	unlikely	possible
7. practically	nearly	carefully
8. react	respond	ignore
9. skip	copy	miss
10. unique	different	similar

ACTIVITY 11 | Collocations

Fill in the blank with the word or phrase that most naturally completes the phrase.

employees	face	factor	flexible	member

1. a(n) _____ approach

2. a(n) _____ of the household

3. _____ challenges

4. prospective _____

5. a(n) _____ in our decision

6. a few _____ ago

7. a caring _____

8. _____ very poor to extremely wealthy

9. _____ one you want

10. classified on the _____ of

ACTIVITY 12 | Word forms

Complete each sentence with the correct word form. Use the correct form of the verbs.

NOUN	VERB	ADJECTIVE	ADVERB	SENTENCES
basis	base	basic	basically	**1.** They _____ their decisions on a wide range of considerations. **2.** Trees can be identified on the _____ of their leaves.
classification	classify	classified		**3.** Students learned about the _____ of plants and animals. **4.** The department _____ students according to their test scores.
generation	generate	generational	generationally	**5.** Some attitudes are _____; the views of younger people are different from their parents'. **6.** The next _____ will probably not have landlines in their homes.

NOUN	VERB	ADJECTIVE	ADVERB	SENTENCES
personality	personalize	personal	personally	**7.** Employees should avoid making _____ calls at work.
				8. One way to _____ your office space is with photos.
replacement	replace	replaceable		**9.** The movie director needs to find a _____ for the role.
				10. Some people _____ their smartphones every year.

ACTIVITY 13 | Vocabulary in writing

Choose five words from Words to Know. Write a complete sentence with each word.

1. _____

2. _____

3. _____

4. _____

5. _____

BUILDING BETTER SENTENCES

ACTIVITY 14 | Error correction

Read the sentences below. Each sentence has one error. Find and correct the errors.

1. Hippos have unusual sweat who turns red when they are upset.

2. The meteorologist's weather predict turned out to be completely wrong.

3. A research suggests that 95 percent of people text things that they would never say.

4. Holding hands while they sleep keep sea otters from drifting apart.

5. Easter Island is famous for their giant statues, which are hundreds of years old.

ACTIVITY 15 | Combining sentences

Combine the ideas into one sentence. You may change the word forms, but do not change or omit any ideas. There may be more than one answer.

1. Elephants have domes.
The domes are on their heads.
African elephants have one dome.
Asian elephants have two domes.

_____

_____

2. Saudi Arabia has no rivers.
The United Arab Emirates has no rivers.
Both have _wadis_.
Wadis are riverbeds.
The riverbeds are often dry.

_____

_____

3. There is a garbage patch.
It is in the Pacific Ocean.
It is full of plastic.
The plastic was brought there by ocean currents.

_____

_____

Plastic and glass marine debris washed ashore in the harbor of a North Pacific island

ACTIVITY 16 | Writing about a photo

Write five to eight sentences about the photo on a separate piece of paper. Make sure that you include at least one subject adjective clause.

Picnic parties fill Ueno Park during cherry blossom season in Tokyo, Japan.

WRITING

ACTIVITY 17 | Choosing a topic

Follow these steps to think about topics you could write about.

1. List at least three things that you know well.

_____

_____

_____

2. List two topics that you are interested in and want to learn about.

_____

_____

3. Choose a topic from the list below or choose one of the topics you are interested in from step 2. This topic will be the subject of your classification essay.

Types of transportation   Types of places to relax

Types of English language classes   Types of video games

Your topic: _____

ACTIVITY 18 | Brainstorming

On a separate piece of paper, brainstorm your topic. Use a method that works for you: listing, making a cluster diagram, or freewriting.

WRITER'S NOTE Thesis Statements

Remember that the thesis statement guides the focus of the essay. There are two types of thesis statements: direct and indirect.

Direct thesis: The main points are clearly stated in the thesis statement.

> Buyers should keep in mind several factors when purchasing a car: price, gas mileage, and functionality.

Indirect thesis: The main points are not stated directly. Instead, they are implied in the thesis statement.

> There are many factors to consider when buying a car.

ACTIVITY 19 | Selecting a purpose and outlining

Follow these steps to prepare your outline.

1. Write a purpose statement for your essay. What information do you want to share with your audience, and why? Start with *The purpose of my essay is to ...*

   _____

   _____

   _____

2. Based on your brainstorming, decide what information you are going to include in your essay and how it will be organized. Then list your three main points of development.

   _____

   _____

   _____

3. Decide if your thesis will be direct or indirect. Write it below and circle the type.

Thesis statement: _____

_____

_____ (direct / indirect)

4. Now write an outline on a separate piece of paper.

5. Exchange outlines with a partner. Use the Peer Editing Form for Outlines in the *Writer's Handbook* to help you comment on your partner's outline. Use your partner's comments to revise your own outline.

ACTIVITY 20 | Writing the first draft

On a separate piece of paper or on a computer, write the first draft of your essay. If you are handwriting your first draft, remember to skip lines because it will be easier for you to make changes. This first draft is not your final draft.

ACTIVITY 21 | Getting feedback from a peer

Exchange first drafts with a partner. Read your partner's draft. Then use Peer Editing Form 4 in the *Writer's Handbook* to help you comment on your partner's writing. Consider your partner's comments as you revise your essay.

ACTIVITY 22 | Reread, rethink, rewrite

Use all the feedback that you have received, including peer feedback, instructor comments, and self-evaluation, to revise your first draft. Then write a final draft on a separate piece of paper.

WRITER'S NOTE Using Transitions

As you revise your essay, see if you can improve the quality and clarity of your writing by adding transition words and phrases. Transitions show the relationships between ideas and improve the flow and coherence of your essay. For more information, see the *Writer's Handbook*.

ACTIVITY 23 | Proofreading the final draft

Use the following checklist to review your final draft. In addition, try reading your essay aloud. When you finish, add a title to your essay.

- ☐ I have a hook in my introduction.
- ☐ My thesis statement gives a clear idea of how the essay will be developed.
- ☐ Each body paragraph has a clear topic sentence.
- ☐ I use subject adjective clauses correctly.
- ☐ My conclusion summarizes the main idea and gives the reader something to think about.

Additional Topics for Writing

Here are five ideas for a classification essay. Choose a topic and follow your teacher's instructions.

TOPIC 1: Classify a collection of something, such as cars or things found in nature, into distinct categories.

TOPIC 2: Classify the most popular college majors (areas of study).

TOPIC 3: Write about different types of ethnic restaurants.

TOPIC 4: Classify parenting styles.

TOPIC 5: Write an essay classifying tourist attractions.

TEST PREP

> **TIP**
>
> When writing an essay, it is important to have a strong thesis statement with a main idea. It may also include the points of development. Remember that if your thesis statement is not clear, the reader will have difficulty following the supporting ideas in the body paragraphs.

You should spend about 40 minutes on this task. Write a five-paragraph essay about the following topic:

Classify friends into three main types.

Include any relevant examples from your own knowledge. Be sure that the points of development are clear. Check for correct use of subject adjective clauses. Write at least 250 words.

5 | Cause-Effect Essays

Plastic Islands, an art exhibit of 60,000 plastic bottles in Cibeles Fountain, Madrid, Spain, was installed to raise awareness of the environmental impact of disposable plastics.

OBJECTIVES
- Understand the organization of a cause-effect essay
- Use different ways to express past actions
- Use prepositions with nouns
- Write a cause-effect essay

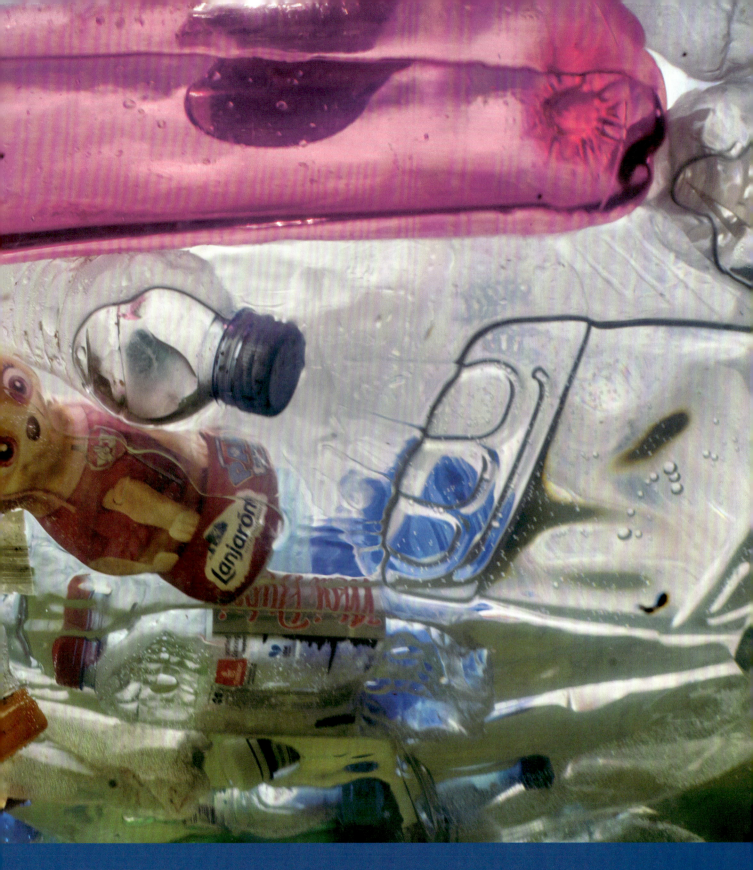

FREEWRITE | Look at the photo and read the caption. What effects do you think the art installation will have on the public? Write your ideas on a separate piece of paper.

ELEMENTS OF GREAT WRITING

What is a Cause-Effect Essay?

Cause-effect essays explain why things happen (causes) and what happens as a result of an action or an event (effects). They can be written to inform or to persuade.

In a cause-effect essay, it is important to choose a topic that fits a cause-effect relationship. In other words, you need to choose a topic and then describe its causes or its effects. Here are some appropriate titles for cause-effect essays:

- The Negative Effects of Internet Use
- The Real Causes of the Spanish-American War
- The Unintended Consequences of Learning a Second Language

The following charts show possible cause and effect relationships.

ONE CAUSE	ONE EFFECT
Sea levels are higher.	Flooding of coastal cities is more frequent.
Driving conditions were poor on May 7, 2018.	Over 20 cars were involved in an accident.
People are living longer.	Increased health care is needed for the elderly.

SEVERAL CAUSES	ONE EFFECT
Marwan takes good notes in class.	
Marwan studies his notes every day.	Marwan gets high scores on his exams.
Marwan participates in class.	

ONE CAUSE	SEVERAL EFFECTS
	The value of the currency decreases.
People lose trust in a country's currency.	Prices on most goods increase.
	Exchange rates for the currency fall.

People enjoying a sunny day at Singapore Marina Barrage Park

ACTIVITY 1 | Choosing appropriate topics

Read these titles. Check (✓) the three that are the most appropriate for a cause-effect essay. Be prepared to give reasons for your choices.

_____ **1.** The Causes of War

_____ **2.** Some Common Reasons for Quitting a Job

_____ **3.** The Beatles: The Greatest Group Ever?

_____ **4.** Types of Restaurant Jobs

_____ **5.** The Impact of High Gasoline Prices

_____ **6.** Summer Vacations vs. Winter Vacations

Organizing a Cause-Effect Essay

Once you have chosen a topic and decided to write about causes and/or effects, you should write an outline for the essay. Here is an example outline for an essay on the effects of weather on people.

Title: How Sunny Weather Affects People

I. Introduction

    A. Hook

    B. Connecting information

    C. Thesis statement: Sunny weather can affect people's moods, activities, and fashion.

II. Body Paragraph 1: Mood

    A. Not trapped inside

    B. Increased melatonin production → better mood and sense of well-being

III. Body Paragraph 2: Activities

    A. Beach

    B. Picnics

    C. Outdoor sports

IV. Body Paragraph 3: Fashion

    A. Lighter-colored clothes

    B. Lighter fabrics, less fabric

V. Conclusion

    A. Restatement of the thesis

    B. Summary of the main points

    C. Concluding sentence with suggestion, prediction, or opinion

(SUPPORT labels appear in the left margin beside Body Paragraphs 1, 2, and 3.)

Supporting Details

In a cause-effect essay, you can organize your supporting ideas in one of three ways:
- by **category**
- in **chronological order**
- by **order of importance**

In the outline on the previous page, the effects of sunshine are organized into three categories: mood, activities, and fashion. The writer can further develop the ideas by adding concrete examples, as shown in section III of the outline below.

III. Body Paragraph 2: Activities

    A. Beach

        1. Warm water ➞ swimming and surfing

        2. Warm sand ➞ volleyball and looking for shells

    B. Picnics

        1. Socializing

        2. Grilling outdoors

    C. Outdoor sports

        1. Individual sports, e.g., golf

        2. Team sports, e.g., soccer, basketball

ACTIVITY 2 | Brainstorming cause-effect ideas

With a partner, brainstorm five harmful effects that social media can have on teenagers' learning and education. Write them on a separate piece of paper. You will use some of these ideas in the next activity.

Teens on their phones at a skateboard park

ACTIVITY 3 | Making an outline for a cause-effect essay

Complete the outline with words and phrases from the box. For Body Paragraph 3, choose three of your ideas from Activity 2, and add them to the outline.

depression	hook	overall health	thesis
eye strain	opinion	psychological	thesis statement

Title: The Harmful Effects of Social Media on Teens

I. Introduction

    A. _____

    B. Connecting information

    C. _____

II. Body Paragraph 1: _____ effects

    A. Antisocial behavior

    B. _____

    C. Aggressive tendencies

III. Body Paragraph 2: Physical effects

    A. Lethargy (no energy)

    B. Reduced activity level and _____

    C. _____

IV. Body Paragraph 3: Educational effects (your ideas)

    A. _____

    B. _____

    C. _____

V. Conclusion

    A. Restate the _____

    B. Summarize the main points

    C. Concluding statement: A suggestion, _____, or prediction

ACTIVITY 4 | Moving from paragraph to essay

The paragraph "Academic Success" from Unit 3 has been expanded into a five-paragraph essay. Notice the similarities in structure and how the three supporting ideas in the paragraph have become main ideas for the body paragraphs in the essay. Read the two texts and answer the questions that follow.

WORDS TO KNOW Essay 5.1

concept: (n) a general idea, often abstract
go over: (v phr) to look at something carefully
implement: (v) to start, put in action

participate in: (v phr) to take part in an activity or event
simply: (adv) without difficulty; only, just
specific: (adj) unlike any other; special

PARAGRAPH 5.1

Academic Success

Most college students hope to achieve academic success, but sometimes they are not sure how to reach this goal. Of course, they know about the importance of note-taking skills and reviewing information before an exam. *However, there are other strategies that can help.* Juan Rodriguez discovered this in a particularly difficult calculus class. *Choosing to sit in the front of the class was one of his strategies.* When he sat there, he paid more attention to the lecture and was more engaged. *Another strategy was previewing the information that the instructor was going to introduce.* Juan would go over the new material the day before the lecture and come to class with an idea of that day's lecture topic. He was more comfortable with the information because it was not new to him. *Finally, Juan found a classmate who was already good at calculus.* By asking for his classmate's help, Juan received different explanations from those of his instructor. Having this "expert" friend who explained difficult math ideas allowed Juan to process calculus more easily. *If a student makes some adjustments to his or her academic habits, as Juan did, he or she will likely be more successful.*

Topic sentence

Support 1

Support 2

Support 3

Conclusion

Academic Success

Introduction

1 Most college students hope to achieve "academic success," but they are not sure how to reach this goal. Of course, they know about the importance of note-taking skills and reviewing information before an exam. However, there are other strategies that can help. Juan Rodriguez discovered this in a particularly difficult calculus class. There are three **specific** strategies that helped him be successful: sitting in the front of the classroom, previewing information, and talking with classmates.

Body paragraph 1

2 Choosing to sit in the front of the class was one of his strategies. He had read that students who sit in the front pay more attention and are more engaged. In addition, professors are more likely to notice the students who sit up front. As a result of being closer to the professor, Juan found that he was more likely to **participate in** class discussions. The best part about this behavior is that it required almost no effort. Juan took the first step toward improving his class performance by **simply** sitting in the front of the classroom each day.

Body paragraph 2

3 Another strategy that led to his increased academic success was previewing the information that the instructor was going to introduce. Juan would **go over** the new material the day before the lecture and come to class with an idea of that day's lecture topic. He was more comfortable with the information because it was not new to him. In addition, by previewing the information, Juan was able to write down questions to ask the teacher in class. Coming to class with an idea of that day's lecture topic and some questions meant that Juan was much more likely to understand the new material.

Body paragraph 3

4 Finally, Juan found a classmate who was already good at calculus. By asking for his classmate's help, Juan received different explanations from those of his instructor. Having this "expert" friend who explained difficult math **concepts** allowed Juan to process the subject more easily. He soon understood terms like *variable* and *coefficient* and was able to work out algebraic problems on his own. **Implementing** this behavior greatly improved Juan's understanding of the subject matter and improved his chances of success in the course.

Conclusion

5 While many college students work hard to achieve academic success, not everyone knows what it takes to reach this goal. Students can learn and use the simple habits of sitting in the front of the classroom, previewing information, and talking with classmates. If a student makes these adjustments to his or her academic habits, as Juan did, he or she will likely be more successful.

1. Are the three points of development about the causes or effects of academic success?

   _____

2. Underline the writer's hook in Essay 5.1. Is it a question, an interesting observation, or a quote?

   _____

3. Underline the thesis statement. Where is it restated in the essay?

   _____

4. Write each cause and each effect.

   a. _sitting in the front of the class_____ ⟶ _____

   b. _____ ⟶ _____

   c. _____ ⟶ _____

5. How does the writer organize the essay: categorically, chronologically, or in order of importance? _____

ACTIVITY 5 | Finding word forms in an essay

Fill in the missing word forms. You can find them in Essay 5.1.

NOUN	VERB	ADJECTIVE	ADVERB
achievement		achievable	Ø
	add	additional	additionally
alternative	alternate		alternatively
discovery		discovered	Ø
	Ø	habitual	habitually
improvement		improved	Ø
simplicity	simplify	simple	
specifics	specify		specifically
	strategize	strategic	strategically
success	succeed		successfully

ACTIVITY 6 | Brainstorming

In Activity 1, you chose three titles for cause-effect essays. Choose one of those titles and write it below. Then brainstorm some ideas for the topic on a separate piece of paper. Use a brainstorming technique such as listing, making a cluster diagram, or freewriting.

Title: _____

ACTIVITY 7 | Developing an outline

With a partner or in a small group, develop a general outline for the essay topic you brainstormed in Activity 6. Fill in the outline.

Title: _____

I. Introduction

Hook: _____

Connecting information: _____

Thesis statement: _____

_____

II. Body Paragraph 1 (Cause or Effect 1): _____

Supporting details: _____

_____

_____

III. Body Paragraph 2 (Cause or Effect 2): _____

Supporting details: _____

_____

_____

IV. Body Paragraph 3 (Cause or Effect 3): _____

Supporting details: _____

_____

_____

V. Conclusion

Concluding statement: _____

_____

Grammar: Common Cause-Effect Structures

Connectors and transition words help show the relationship between a cause and an effect. Study these common cause-effect structures.

WITHIN A SENTENCE	
CONNECTOR	**EXAMPLES**
because of + noun	The city flooded **because of** the storm.
because + subject + verb	Elephants are in danger **because** hunters kill them for their ivory.
one/another cause of/reason for	Bad weather was **another reason for** the delay.
due to + noun	Many people lost their homes **due to** the hurricane.
subject + verb, **so** subject + verb	The election results were very close, **so** they recounted the votes.
subject + verb **so (that)** subject + verb	The company raised starting salaries **so that** it could attract better job applicants.
BETWEEN SENTENCES	
TRANSITION	**EXAMPLES**
As a result, **Therefore,** subject + verb **Because of this,**	Sea levels are rising. **As a result,** coastal cities flood more often. Children spend too much time indoors. **Therefore,** they do not get enough exercise or vitamin D.

ACTIVITY 8 | Using connectors and transitions

Complete the sentences with your own ideas.

1. The need for computer engineers is growing, so universities _____
   _____ .

2. Because of _____, student scores on reading tests are declining.

3. Snowstorms can be very dangerous. Therefore, _____
   _____ .

4. More young athletes are getting injured due to _____
   _____ .

5. Too much sun exposure can cause cancer. Another cause of cancer is _____
   _____ .

6. Adolescents use social media a lot, so _____
   _____ .

7. The economy is improving. As a result, _____
   _____ .

Grammar: Ways of Expressing Past Events

Study the four verb forms that indicate past events or situations.

EXPLANATION	EXAMPLES
Use the **simple past** for an action that is complete.	Because she **worked** so hard, her business **became** very successful. **worked** = regular **became** = irregular
Use the **past progressive** for an action that was in progress in the past and was interrupted by another action. The interruption is usually in the **simple past**.	I **was studying** for my final exam when I **got** the terrible news. **was studying** = past progressive (action) **got** the terrible news = simple past (interruption)

The **present perfect** describes two kinds of past actions:
  a. an action that began in the past and continues now
  b. a completed action that is important to the current situation or discussion
  c. a repeated action before now
	a. These people **have lived** in this area for almost a century.
	b. Many citizens are upset because the government **has increased** taxes.
	c. They **have protested** three times this year.

Use the **past perfect** when there are two past actions in order to show clearly which one happened first. The earlier action is in the past perfect, and the later action is usually in the **simple past**. Note: This form is used much less than the simple past.	Dinosaurs **had disappeared** long before humans **appeared** on Earth. **had disappeared** = past perfect (first action) **appeared** = simple past (second action)

ACTIVITY 9 | Noticing past verbs

With a partner, read these sentences and underline the verbs. Discuss why each verb form was used.

1. Zach was giving his presentation when his cell phone went off.

2. Dr. Silva researched the connection between stress and health until she retired.

3. The increase in housing construction has created a number of new jobs.

4. The online sale had already ended by the time Emir decided to purchase the tablet.

5. There have been several days of record heat this year.

ACTIVITY 10 | Using past verbs

Complete the sentences with your own ideas and a past verb.

1. Because the storm lasted several days, _____ .

2. Before the flight took off, the flight crew _____ .

3. Kayla _____ when she heard the news.

4. No one knows how many people _____ .

5. Since the turn of the century, _____ .

ACTIVITY 11 | Practicing with present and past verbs

Read the following paragraph. Then underline the correct verbs in parentheses.

> **WORDS TO KNOW** Paragraph 5.2
>
> **allow:** (v) to let, permit
> **benefit:** (v) to help
> **deadly:** (adj) fatal; dangerous enough to cause death
>
> **economy:** (n) the economic conditions on a worldwide, national, or regional scale
> **result in:** (v phr) to cause
> **tremendous:** (adj) huge; vast

PARAGRAPH 5.2

The Positive Impact[1] of the Panama Canal

Despite the **tremendous** amount of time and money it cost to build, the Panama Canal [1] (has / had / was) greatly **benefited** society. Firstly, the opening of the Panama Canal **allowed** a rapid growth of the world **economy**. The canal provided much faster and safer shipping routes to and from many countries. This [2] (leads / led / had led) to a significant decrease in the cost of goods. Using the canal also **resulted in** far fewer deaths at sea. Previously, ships wanting to go from one side of the Americas to the other [3] (need / needed / has needed) to navigate south around Cape Horn, which is known for its **deadly** waters. Finally, Panama's economy [4] (grew / was growing / has grown) since the opening of the canal. Panama has collected fees from each ship that passes through the canal and has created jobs for its citizens. Since it was opened in 1914, the Panama Canal [5] (has / had / has had) a positive impact on the global economy and the citizens of Panama.

[1]impact: an effect

A cruise ship in port in the Panama Canal

Noun and Preposition Combinations

Study the following common combinations of prepositions and nouns.

NOUN + PREPOSITION COMBINATIONS			
of	**for**	**in**	**on, to**
cost of (oil)	application for (a job)	belief in (progress)	effect on (quality)
lack of (sleep)	demand for (action)	change in (policy)	information on (banks)
limitations of (the law)	need for (change)	decrease in (prices)	report on (technology)
means of (deciding)	preference for (sweets)	experience in (law)	alternative to (gas)
source of (energy)	reason for (failure)	increase in (cost)	invitation to (an event)
state of (the economy)	request for (a book)	interest in (science)	reaction to (a problem)

PREPOSITION + NOUN COMBINATIONS			
out of	**for**	**in**	**at, by, under, with**
out of control	for dinner	in a hurry	at (the same) time
out of date	for example	in fact	by hand
out of money	for future reference	in order	by mistake
out of order	for sale	in other words	under control
out of time	for the record	in reality	under pressure
out of touch	for your information	in the beginning	with reference to

ACTIVITY 12 | Using noun and preposition combinations

Write the preposition that best completes each sentence.

PARAGRAPH 5.3

The Unforeseen[1] Impact of Air Conditioning

Most people agree that there is a huge need **1** _____ air conditioning in the modern world. **2** _____ the same time, however, behavioral scientists are concerned about the negative effects that air conditioning has had **3** _____ society in general. To be sure, air conditioning has been beneficial, but what has the cost **4** _____ this benefit been? First of all, people do not get outside as much as they used to because of the comfort of air-conditioned homes. As a result, they are not getting as much fresh air and sunshine. Second, there has been a decrease **5** _____ the amount of exercise that people are getting. On some days, they do not even step outside, which means that they are, **6** _____ fact, doing a lot less exercising. Finally, the invention of air conditioning has led to longer working hours as employers expect more productivity in a cool, comfortable work space. In sum, air conditioning might not be as positive as it first appeared.

[1]unforeseen: not predicted or expected

ACTIVITY 13 | Previewing a cause-effect essay

Discuss the questions. Then read Essay 5.2, "The Benefits of a Healthy Lifestyle," presented in the paragraphs in Activities 14–17.

1. *Lifestyle* refers to the habits and patterns of how a person lives. Name four features of a healthy lifestyle.

_____

_____

2. Can a positive social life contribute to your health? How?

_____

ACTIVITY 14 | Selecting a hook

Read the introductory paragraph and select the best hook. Write it on the lines. Be prepared to explain your choice.

> **WORDS TO KNOW** Essay 5.2
>
> **a good deal of:** (phr) a lot of
> **aware:** (adj) having knowledge of
> **confidence:** (n) belief in one's abilities
> **lifestyle:** (n) the manner in which one lives
> **pattern:** (n) a repeated set of events or features
>
> **pursue:** (v) to chase; to work hard at
> **risk:** (n) a chance; a danger of losing something
> **satisfying:** (adj) making one happy
> **transform:** (v) to change from one shape or condition to another

ESSAY 5.2

The Benefits of a Healthy Lifestyle

1 _____

_____

This is as true today as it was in the past. Unfortunately, many people are not **aware** of the effects their diet can have on how they feel. Likewise, they are unaware of the benefits of a regular exercise routine. In fact, there are physical, psychological, and social benefits to living a healthy **lifestyle**.

a. According to Mark Twain, "the only way to keep your health is to eat what you don't want, drink what you don't like, and do what you'd rather not."

b. Exercise is one of the best and fastest ways of promoting overall health.

c. Is it possible that a few simple changes could lead to a better life?

ACTIVITY 15 | Using connectors and transitions

Complete the sentences with the connectors in the box. Look carefully at the sentence structure to help you choose the correct word(s).

also	another	for instance	in addition	so that	thus

ESSAY 5.2 (CONT.)

2   A person can enjoy physical benefits from choosing to follow a healthy lifestyle. [1] _____, proper exercise and a well-balanced diet help a person to maintain a slim, athletic figure. Countless studies have shown that a regular exercise routine significantly reduces the **risk** of almost every major disease. Healthy habits [2] _____ give people more energy [3] _____ they can see more, do more, and experience more from life. [4] _____, people who maintain a healthy lifestyle will, on average, live longer than people who do not take care of their health. [5] _____ physical benefit that people notice is healthier-looking skin. [6] _____, a person can gain many physical benefits from maintaining a healthy lifestyle.

A large yoga event at the Grand Palais in Paris, France

ACTIVITY 16 | Editing for errors

Paragraph 3 has five errors: article (1), word form (1), subject-verb agreement (2), and unclear pronoun reference (1). Find and correct them.

ESSAY 5.2 (CONT.)

3   People who take care of themselves enjoy psychological beneficial. For example, regular exercise produces endorphins, which are the body's natural way to lift one's mood. Better nutrition means that they are also better equipped to deal with the stress of day-to-day life. Because of the effects that their healthy choices has on their bodies, people with the healthy lifestyle generally feel better about themselves. Most importantly, people who takes care of themselves agree that they feel better about themselves because they have more self-**confidence**.

Paragraph 4 has seven errors: article (2), word form (1), subject-verb agreement (2), and verb form (2). Find and correct them.

ESSAY 5.2 (CONT.)

4   Taking proper care of one's health also leads to better social life. The confidence that a person gains from feeling healthy and in shape improve his or her social and business relationships. Because health-minded people engage in a variety of physical activities, they had increased their chances of meeting other people. For example, many people makes friends at the locally gym. Similarly, someone who goes to beach frequently to play volleyball greatly increases his or her chances of meeting people. Since people who **pursue** a healthy lifestyle were feeling better about themselves, they are more likely to have **satisfying** social lives.

ACTIVITY 17 | Using correct grammar

Underline the correct word or phrase in parentheses.

5   It certainly ¹ (makes / had made) sense ² (to / for) live a healthy lifestyle; the benefits ³ (were / are) clear. Although ⁴ (changing / changed) one's eating and exercising **patterns** may be difficult at first, it becomes easier with time. People ⁵ (do not / did not) have to start by changing ⁶ (their / his) whole lives; they can start by making small changes each day or each week ⁷ (until / before) they have **transformed** themselves. ⁸ (While / After) pursuing a ⁹ (health / healthy) lifestyle may require **a good deal of** time and energy, the physical, psychological, and social benefits ¹⁰ (are / have been) well worth the effort.

ACTIVITY 18 | Analyzing the essay

Answer these questions about Essay 5.2.

1. What are the three points of development given in the introductory paragraph?

    _____

    _____

2. Does the writer tell about causes or effects? _____

3. In Paragraph 2, the writer discusses some physical benefits of a healthy lifestyle. List three of the benefits here:

    a. _____

    b. _____

    c. _____

4. How does the writer organize the essay: categorically, chronologically, or in order of

    importance? _____

5. Underline the thesis statement. Where is the thesis restated?

    _____

BUILDING BETTER VOCABULARY

ACTIVITY 19 | Word associations

Circle the word or phrase that is more closely related to the bold word or phrase on the left.

1.	aware	knowledgeable about	ignorant
2.	concept	general idea	detail
3.	deadly	very helpful	very dangerous
4.	participate in	a discussion	a rule
5.	pursue	work hard at	discover
6.	result in	effect	cause
7.	risk	danger	pleasure
8.	simply	only	completely
9.	transform	different	similar
10.	tremendous	small	huge

ACTIVITY 20 | Collocations

Fill in the blank with the word or phrase that most naturally completes the phrase.

confidence	go over	participate in	satisfying	transform

1. _____ the test results

2. completely _____ one's appearance

3. a _____ meal

4. have _____

5. _____ sports

| healthy | implement | pattern | risk | specific |

6. a(n) _____ of behavior

7. lower the _____ of disease

8. follow _____ instructions

9. _____ some changes

10. a(n) _____ lifestyle

ACTIVITY 21 | Word forms

Complete each sentence with the correct word form. Use the correct form of the verbs.

NOUN	VERB	ADJECTIVE	ADVERB	SENTENCES
concept	conceive	conceptual	conceptually	**1.** The marketing team has a strong _____ for their campaign. **2.** The artist's work is very _____ ; not everyone understands it.
confidence	confide	confident	confidently	**3.** Good public speakers demonstrate _____ . **4.** Researchers are _____ that they will find a genetic cause.
implementation	implement	implemented		**5.** Next year, the administration will _____ the new policy. **6.** They expect full _____ to take at least six months.
participation/ participant	participate	participating		**7.** How many adults _____ in a sport at least once a week? **8.** Class _____ is an important part of one's overall grade.
risk	risk	risky		**9.** If you do not proofread, you _____ submitting a paper with errors. **10.** Unfortunately, some medical procedures are quite _____ .

ACTIVITY 22 | Vocabulary in writing

Choose five words from Words to Know. Write a complete sentence with each word.

1. _____

2. _____

3. _____

4. _____

5. _____

BUILDING BETTER SENTENCES

ACTIVITY 23 | Scrambled sentences

Unscramble the words and phrases to write complete sentences.

1. a great deal of / thought / requires / deciding on / careful / a job offer

_____

2. healthy diets / people / bad habits / implemented / go back to / who have / sometimes

_____

3. use / specific strategies / research / on tests / who / shows that / do better / students

_____

4. was suffering / natural disasters / because of / a series of / the economy

_____

5. offered / the decrease / due to / on the exam / the college / study sessions / in passing scores

_____

ACTIVITY 24 | Combining sentences

Combine the ideas into one sentence. You may change the word forms, but do not change or omit any ideas. There may be more than one answer.

1. Many American adults are obese.
This raises their risk of heart disease.
It also raises the risk of diabetes.

_____

_____

2. A hundred and fifty whales got stranded on a beach.
The beach was in Australia.
Rescuers could not reach them.
The weather was very bad.
There were a large number of sharks.

_____

_____

3. U.S. banks had made many loans.
The loans were risky.
They lost a lot of money.
This happened in 2008.

_____

_____

ACTIVITY 25 | Writing sentences

Read the pairs of words. Write an original sentence using the words listed.

1. (aware / danger) _____

2. (specific / plan) _____

3. (pursue / career) _____

4. (tremendous / opportunity) _____

5. (implement / lifestyle) _____

WRITING

ACTIVITY 26 | Brainstorming a topic

Choose a topic from this list for a cause-effect essay. Brainstorm ideas about your topic on a separate piece of paper. Then circle your best ideas.

- The effects of reality television on society
- The main reasons that animals become endangered
- Three major reasons why people stop being friends
- The effects of being bilingual
- The positive effects of nuclear energy

ACTIVITY 27 | Selecting a purpose and outlining

Follow these steps to prepare your outline.

1. Write a purpose statement for your essay. What is its purpose? What information do you want to share with your audience, and why?

   _____

   _____

2. Based on your brainstorming, list your three main points of development.

   a. _____

   b. _____

   c. _____

3. Decide if you will focus on causes or effects. Write a thesis statement. _____

   _____

   _____

4. Write an outline on a piece of paper. Refer to the outline in Activity 3 if needed.

5. Exchange outlines with a partner. Use the Peer Editing Form for Outlines in the *Writer's Handbook* to help you comment on your partner's outline. Use your partner's comments to revise your own outline.

ACTIVITY 28 | Writing and revising

Follow these steps to write and revise your essay.

1. On a separate piece of paper, write the first draft of your essay. Use your outline from Activity 27.

2. Exchange first drafts with a partner. Read your partner's draft. Use Peer Editing Form 5 in the *Writer's Handbook* to help you comment on your partner's draft. Consider your partner's comments as you revise your work.

3. Revise your first draft. Use all of the feedback that you have received, including peer feedback and instructor comments, as you revise. Check to make sure that you use correct vocabulary, correct punctuation, and clear language in your essay. When you finish, add an appropriate title to your essay.

4. Use the checklist below to proofread your work.

☐ I have a good hook to start my introduction.
☐ My thesis statement contains a clear topic.
☐ Each body paragraph has a clear topic sentence.
☐ My thoughts and ideas are organized clearly in each paragraph.
☐ I used verb forms correctly.
☐ The concluding paragraph restates the thesis and the main points of development.

Additional Topics for Writing

Here are five topics for a cause-effect essay. Choose a topic and follow your teacher's instructions.

TOPIC 1: Look at the photo at the beginning of this unit. Discuss the causes or effects of waste in our waters.

TOPIC 2: Tell about the effects the invention of email has had on society.

TOPIC 3: Discuss possible reasons why some people are more generous than others. (causes)

TOPIC 4: What makes a person successful? (causes)

TOPIC 5: Discuss the positive effects of extracurricular activities on students.

TEST PREP

> **TIP**
>
> When writing for a test, make sure that your language is specific. You want to show that you have thought about the topic and provided interesting information in your writing. When possible, avoid general words such as *nice*, *thing*, and *very*.

You should spend about 40 minutes on this task. Write a five-paragraph essay about the following topic:

Discuss some of the positive effects of music.

Write a short introduction (with a thesis statement), three body paragraphs, and a conclusion. Include any relevant examples from your own knowledge. Make sure that your points of development are clear. Check for correct use of verb forms. Write at least 250 words.

6 | Comparison Essays

OBJECTIVES
- Understand the organization of a comparison essay
- Use the comparative and superlative of adjectives and adverbs
- Use parallel structure
- Write a comparison essay

A tulip field contrasts sharply with an industrial area in the Netherlands.

FREEWRITE | Look at the photo and read the caption. On a separate piece of paper, list the various ways that the tulip field contrasts with the industrial area.

ELEMENTS OF GREAT WRITING

What Is a Comparison Essay?

A **comparison essay** is one of the most common forms of essay writing. In a comparison essay, the writer discusses the similarities and/or differences between two subjects.

Even though this kind of writing is called "comparison," it is possible to focus on only comparison (similarities), only contrast (differences), or comparison and contrast (similarities and differences).

Choosing Subjects to Compare

In an effective essay of this type, the writer discusses two subjects that do not appear to be similar but are presented in a way that readers can see the not-so-obvious similarities. It is also possible to do the opposite—pointing out the hidden differences between two subjects that appear similar on the surface. Either way, the writer makes the reader think about the two subjects in a new, deeper way.

Here are some appropriate topics for comparison essays:

- watching movies at the theater or at home
- hybrid vs. conventional cars
- breakfast dishes in Japan and China

ACTIVITY 1 | Choosing appropriate comparison topics

Read these titles. Check (✓) the three that are the most appropriate for a comparison essay. Be prepared to explain your choices.

_____ **1.** Why People Should Be Vegetarians

_____ **2.** Laptop and Desktop Computers

_____ **3.** Reducing Your Electricity Usage

_____ **4.** Growing Up as an Only Child or Growing Up with Siblings

_____ **5.** Male and Female Bosses

_____ **6.** Writing a Successful Résumé

Organizing a Comparison Essay

You can organize a comparison essay in two ways: the **block method** or the **point-by-point method**. Regardless of the method you use, you must choose **points of comparison** to compare and/or contrast. For example, if your two subjects are life in London in 1900 and life in London in 2000, you might include three points of comparison: population, technology, and transportation.

Block Method

In the **block method**, you discuss points of comparison about one subject first before discussing the same points about the other subject. It is important to discuss the points of comparison in the same order. Here is an example of an outline using the block method.

Title: Snapshots of London: 1900 and 2000

I. Introduction

    A. Hook

    B. Connecting information

    C. Thesis statement: Though London in 1900 was quite different from London in 2000, important similarities existed in population, technology, and transportation.

II. Body Paragraph 1: London in 1900

    A. Point of comparison 1: population

    B. Point of comparison 2: technology

    C. Point of comparison 3: transportation

III. Body Paragraph 2: London in 2000

    A. Point of comparison 1: population

    B. Point of comparison 2: technology

    C. Point of comparison 3: transportation

IV. Conclusion

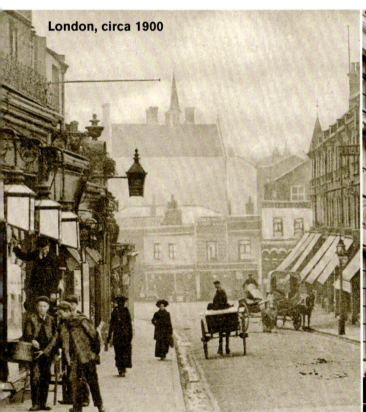

London, circa 1900

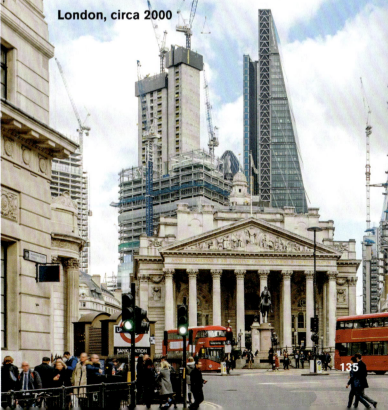

London, circa 2000

135

Point-by-Point Method

In the **point-by-point method**, you discuss one point of comparison for both subjects first before discussing the second and third points of comparison. (You must use at least two points of comparison.) Because information about both subjects is included in each paragraph, the comparison or contrast is easier for the reader to follow. Be sure to discuss the subjects in the same order for each point of comparison. Here is an outline using the point-by-point method.

Title: Snapshots of London: 1900 and 2000

I. Introduction

   A. Hook

   B. Connecting information

   C. Thesis statement: Though London in 1900 was quite different from London in 2000, important similarities existed in population, technology, and transportation.

II. Body Paragraph 1 (Point of comparison 1): Population

   A. London in 1900

   B. London in 2000

SUPPORT

III. Body Paragraph 2 (Point of comparison 2): Technology

   A. London in 1900

   B. London in 2000

SUPPORT

IV. Body Paragraph 3 (Point of comparison 3): Transportation

   A. London in 1900

   B. London in 2000

SUPPORT

V. Conclusion

Supporting Details

The essay "Snapshots of London: 1900 and 2000" will have supporting sentences for each point of comparison. However, where those sentences appear in the essay will depend on the method of organization. For example, on the next page, notice the location of the highlighted details generated to support *technology*.

BLOCK METHOD	POINT-BY-POINT METHOD
Snapshots of London: 1900 and 2000	**Snapshots of London: 1900 and 2000**
I. Introduction	I. Introduction
II. London in 1900	II. Population
A. Population	**A.** London in 1900
B. Technology	**B.** London in 2000
1. lighting	III. Technology
2. heating	**A.** London in 1900
3. transatlantic communication systems	**1.** lighting
C. Transportation	**2.** heating
III. London in 2000	**3.** transatlantic communication systems
A. Population	**B.** London in 2000
B. Technology	**1.** lighting
1. lighting	**2.** heating
2. heating	**3.** transatlantic communication systems
3. transatlantic communication systems	IV. Transportation
C. Transportation	**A.** London in 1900
IV. Conclusion	**B.** London in 2000
	V. Conclusion

ACTIVITY 2 | Making an outline for a comparison essay

Complete the outline with words and phrases from the box below.

Chicago	hurricanes	Miami
comparison	introduction	names
effects	location	temperature

Title: The Weather in Chicago and Miami

I. _____

II. Body Paragraph 1 (Point of comparison 1): The number of seasons

  A. Chicago

    1. Location

    2. Number and names of seasons

  B. Miami

    1. _____

    2. Number and _____ of seasons

SUPPORT

III. Body Paragraph 2 (Point of comparison 2): The extreme temperatures

A. _____

　1. Worst season

　2. Supporting fact: temperature

B. _____

　1. Worst season

　2. Supporting fact: _____

IV. Body Paragraph 3 (Point of _____ 3): Severe weather conditions

A. Chicago

　1. Blizzard

　2. When blizzards occur

　3. _____ of a blizzard

B. Miami

　1. Hurricane

　2. When _____ occur

　3. Effects of a hurricane

V. Conclusion

ACTIVITY 3 | Expanding a paragraph into an essay

Paragraph 6.1 has been expanded into Essay 6.1. Connect similar portions of the paragraph and essay using lines or different-colored highlighters. Then answer the questions that follow.

> **WORDS TO KNOW** Essay 6.1
>
> **constant:** (adj) happening all the time; continuous
> **constitute:** (v) to make up, compose
> **frigid:** (adj) freezing, very cold
> **humidity:** (n) the amount of moisture in the air
> **illustrate:** (v) to give examples, explain
> **paralyze:** (v) to cause a loss of the ability to move or function
>
> **preference:** (n) liking one thing more than another
> **resident:** (n) a person who lives in a certain area
> **severe:** (adj) very strong
> **threat:** (n) a danger
> **unbearable:** (adj) so painful or difficult that one cannot continue
> **urban:** (adj) related to the city

The Weather in Chicago and Miami

Both Chicago and Miami are very popular cities, but their climates could not be more different. The first difference is the seasons. Chicago has all four seasons, but Miami does not. People in Chicago enjoy very different weather in the summer, fall, winter, and spring. Miami, in contrast, has only two seasons: a very mild winter and a very long summer. Another major difference in the weather between these two cities is that Chicago's worst weather occurs in the winter. On average, the high temperature reaches only around 32 degrees Fahrenheit (0 degrees Celsius), and the low each night goes down to about 20 degrees (-7 degrees Celsius). Unlike Chicago, the problem in Miami is not the cold but rather the heat. In the summer, the daytime temperature reaches 95 degrees Fahrenheit (35 degrees Celsius) and drops to only 75 (24) or so at night. Finally, people in Miami worry about different weather problems. While a blizzard is the biggest fear for residents of Chicago, the biggest weather problem for people in Miami is a hurricane. In sum, these two cities experience very different weather.

The Weather in Chicago and Miami

1   What **constitutes** a desirable climate to live in? One person's idea of a good climate may easily be another person's weather nightmare[1]. Two U.S. cities that **illustrate** this are Chicago and Miami, large **urban** areas whose climates could not be more different.

2   The first difference is the number of seasons. Chicago, which is located in the midwestern part of the United States, has four seasons: summer, fall, winter, and spring. These seasons are marked by distinct weather changes. Miami, on the other hand, is in the Southeast. Because it is much farther south and by the Atlantic Ocean, the climate is much warmer. Miami has two seasons: a mild winter and a long, hot summer.

3   Another difference is the extreme temperatures in both cities. The worst weather in Chicago occurs in the winter. On average, the high temperature reaches around 32 degrees Fahrenheit (0 degrees Celsius), and the low goes down to about 20 degrees F (-7 degrees C). Frequent high winds make the temperature seem even colder. This combination of cold and wind, called the wind chill factor, can make life almost **unbearable** during the winter. The challenge in Miami is not the cold but rather the heat. In the summer, the temperature reaches 95 degrees F (35 degrees C) in the daytime and drops to only 75 F (24 C) or so at night. Combined with a **constant humidity** of 90 percent or more, the temperature feels much warmer.

4   Finally, Chicago and Miami have different kinds of **severe** weather. Chicago's biggest weather challenge is blizzards, which occur during the **frigid** winter months. When a blizzard hits the city, five or six feet (1.5 or 1.8 meters) of snow can fall. The cold and snow **paralyze** the city, making it impossible for people to go to school or work. On the other hand, the biggest weather problem in Miami is hurricanes. These powerful storms occur from May through November. While hurricanes occur less frequently than blizzards, they can cause more damage. For instance, Hurricane Katrina, which struck Miami and New Orleans in 2005, caused $108 billion in damage.

5   It is clear that each city's climate is different. Chicago **residents** enjoy four distinct seasons, but they have to live with extreme cold and blizzards that can upset their daily routines. Conversely, people in Miami may enjoy warm temperatures, but they have to deal with the **threat** of hurricanes. Although some kinds of weather are easier to live with than others, "the perfect climate" is a matter of personal **preference**.

[1]nightmare: a frightening dream; a terrible experience

Miami Beach, Florida

1. What is the purpose of this essay? Begin your sentence with *The purpose of . . .*

   _____

   _____

2. Which method of organization does the writer use: point-by-point or block?

   _____

3. Circle the writer's hook. What kind of hook is it? _____

4. Underline the thesis statement. Is the thesis restated in the conclusion?

   _____

   If yes, underline that sentence (or sentences).

5. Underline the topic sentence for each body paragraph. How do the topic sentences relate to the thesis statement?

   _____

   _____

6. Reread the concluding paragraph. Does the writer offer a suggestion, an opinion, or

   a prediction? _____

ACTIVITY 4 | Brainstorming and outlining practice

In Activity 1, you identified three titles for comparison essays. Choose one of those titles and brainstorm ideas for the topic on a piece of paper. Then with a partner or on your own, develop a general outline for an essay using the outline below.

Title: _____

Organizational method: _____

I. Introduction

   Thesis statement: _____

   _____

II. Body Paragraph 1 (Point of comparison 1): _____

SUPPORT

   _____

   _____

   _____

III. Body Paragraph 2 (Point of comparison 2): _____

SUPPORT

   _____

   _____

   _____

IV. Body Paragraph 3 (Point of comparison 3): _____

SUPPORT

   _____

   _____

   _____

V. Conclusion

   Concluding statement: _____

   _____

Connectors and Transitions

Study some common connectors and transitions for comparing and contrasting structures.

COMPARING	
BETWEEN SENTENCES	**EXAMPLES**
In addition, . . . Similarly, . . . Likewise, . . .	San Francisco has a mild climate with wet winters and dry summers. **Similarly,** Sydney's winters are quite mild.
WITHIN A SENTENCE	**EXAMPLES**
compared to + noun **the same** + noun + **as** **as** + adjective / adverb + **as** **like** + noun **not only** _____ **but also** _____ **both** _____ **and** _____ Subject + verb, **and** subject + verb, **too**	Tokyo is very large **compared to** Kyoto. Manila has **the same** climate **as** Singapore. Are self-driving cars **as** safe **as** regular cars? Boston is **like** a large town. People **not only** ski, **but also** skate in Austria. **Both** Dallas **and** Austin have hot climates. China is a producer of rice, **and** India is **too.**
CONTRASTING	
BETWEEN SENTENCES	**EXAMPLES**
Conversely, . . . However, . . . On one hand, . . . On the other hand, . . . In contrast, . . . Nevertheless, . . .	Dubai has some of the tallest skyscrapers in the world. **Conversely,** the buildings in Muscat are 10 stories or fewer. Most residents drive to work. **Nevertheless,** there is a growing number who ride bikes.
WITHIN A SENTENCE	**EXAMPLES**
Although / Whereas / While + subject + verb Subject + verb, **but** subject + verb **Unlike** + noun	**Although** London relied on coal for energy in 1900, by 2000 coal provided only nine percent of its energy. Miami has a warm winter, **but** Chicago's winter is cold. **Unlike** most countries, Bhutan was closed off to the world until the late 20th century.

ACTIVITY 5 | Using connectors and transitions

Choose two cities. Write sentences using the connector or transition given.

1. Both _____ and _____

_____.

2. _____

Conversely, _____.

3. While _____

_____.

4. _____

On the other hand, _____ .

5. _____

Similarly, _____ .

Grammar: The Comparative and Superlative

ADJECTIVES	
EXPLANATION	**EXAMPLES**
For one-syllable adjectives, add -er and -est to form the comparative and superlative forms. For two-syllable adjectives ending in -y, change the y to i, and add -er / -est.	Washington, DC, is **cold** in the winter. Boston is **colder** than Washington, DC. Quebec City is **the coldest**. Sudan is **sunnier** than Iceland.
Exceptions include *good / better / the best* and *bad / worse / the worst*.	Chicken is **better** than beef for a healthy heart, but salmon may be **the best** of all.
Adjectives of more than one syllable are preceded by *more* and *the most* to form the comparative and superlative.	Venice is **more beautiful** than Rome. Florence is **the most beautiful** city in Italy.
ADVERBS	
EXPLANATION	**EXAMPLES**
One-syllable adverbs follow the same rule as one-syllable adjectives.	The Shanghai Maglev train travels **fast**. The high-speed TGV train in France goes **faster**. The SCMaglev train in Japan goes **the fastest**.
Adverbs that end in -ly are preceded by *more* and *the most*.	Compared to fruits, people digest vegetables **slowly**. People digest meat **more slowly** than vegetables. We digest fats **the most slowly** of all foods.
EQUALITY	
as + adjective / adverb + *as* *the same* + noun + *as*	The weather in Moscow is **as extreme as** Chicago's. Cricket has **the same number** of players **as** soccer.

The Shanghai Maglev train on the way to Pudong International Airport in China

ACTIVITY 6 | Practice with comparatives and superlatives

Write the correct comparative or superlative form of the word in parentheses.

1. Some people think Lionel Messi is a _____ (good) soccer player than Cristiano Ronaldo.

2. A football field is _____ (long) than a tennis court.

3. Chess has _____ (difficult) rules than checkers does.

4. The _____ (hot) place in the United States is Death Valley, California.

5. A birthday party is usually _____ (casual) than a wedding.

6. The final exam ended _____ (quickly) than everyone anticipated.

7. The _____ (impressive) highway system in the world is Germany's Autobahn.

8. The _____ (bad) cup of coffee Miguel has ever tasted was in the university cafeteria.

9. Aomori City in Japan is the world's _____ (snowy) city.

10. Australia is roughly _____ (same) size as the United States.

Grammar: Parallel Structure

When a sentence includes a list, words in the list should be the same part of speech. Use two or more nouns, adjectives, or verbs, but do not mix these parts of speech.

> Though London in 1900 was quite different from London in 2000, important similarities existed in <u>population</u>, <u>employment</u>, and <u>transportation</u>. (three nouns)

> Summers in Miami are <u>long</u>, <u>hot</u>, and <u>humid</u>. (three adjectives)

Phrases and clauses in a list should also be parallel.

> Survey results can be misleading because there is a huge difference between <u>what people think they do</u> and <u>what they actually do</u>. (two noun clauses)

> Sweden is a family-friendly country because of its <u>paid parental leave</u>, <u>generous monthly payments for children</u>, and <u>free preschool education</u>. (three noun phrases)

> To prepare for a test, students should <u>review their notes</u>, <u>find a study partner</u>, and <u>get a good night's sleep</u>. (three verb phrases)

ACTIVITY 7 | Parallel structure

Complete the sentences using parallel structure.

1. To host a large sporting event such as the World Cup Final, a city needs to have good facilities, _____, and _____.

2. The best vacation spots provide a beautiful setting and _____.

3. While coastal cities have to worry about rising sea levels and beach erosion, inland cities worry more about _____ and _____.

4. In summer, temperatures rise, crops grow, and workers take vacations. In winter, _____, _____, and _____.

5. Students who _____, _____, and _____ generally get high grades.

6. _____ is a great city because of its _____, _____, and _____.

ACTIVITY 8 | Using comparatives, superlatives, and parallel structure

If an underlined part of a sentence below is incorrect, write a correction above it.

1. The most expensive items in this company's budget are employee salaries, communication costs, and spend money on office supplies.

2. Without a doubt, Cairo gets more visitors per year than Sharm el Sheikh does.

3. The car was going as fast as the truck was, but the car had an accident because it turned the corner more sharply the truck.

4. When someone travels to a new city for the first time, the importantest things he or she needs are a clean place to stay, good food to eat, and enough money to get both of these.

5. Some doctors believe that it is most healthy to eat several small meals each day than it is to eat one large meal.

6. Compared to New York City, Paris has more green space, a lower skyline, and good public transportation.

ACTIVITY 9 | Choosing a hook

Essay 6.2 is divided into three sections. Read the introduction paragraph and choose the best hook. Write it on the lines. Be prepared to explain your choice.

> **WORDS TO KNOW** Essay 6.2
>
> **accomplish:** (v) to achieve
> **freedom:** (n) being able to do things without restriction
> **motion:** (n) movement
> **original:** (n) the first version of something
> **principle:** (n) a rule; a standard
>
> **procedure:** (n) a detailed method of doing something
> **remarkably:** (adv) in a noticeable manner
> **spin:** (v) to turn around in a circle or cause something to do so

ESSAY 6.2

Flying a Model Plane vs. a Real Plane

1 _____

_____

Many people dream of doing this, but flying is an expensive hobby. However, people who fly model planes can appreciate the wonder of flight. Using remote-controlled model planes, they can enjoy the **freedom** of taking off in a plane and soaring through the sky. In fact, the experience of flying a model airplane is **remarkably** similar to piloting a real plane.

    a. Have you ever wondered what it would be like to pilot a plane?

    b. Someone said, "Flying in an airplane is mostly boring, but sometimes frightening."

    c. There were many certified pilots in the United States last year.

A man flies a model airplane in Tuscany, Italy.

ACTIVITY 10 | Using connectors and transitions

Read Paragraphs 2 and 3 of Essay 6.2. Complete the sentences with the connectors and transitions in the box. Look carefully at the sentence structure to help you choose the correct word(s).

also	as	even though	in addition
another	both	for example	instance

ESSAY 6.2 (CONT.)

2 [1] _____ people prepare their model airplanes for flight, they are aware that the procedures are the same as the pre-flight **procedures** that pilots follow. [2] _____ model planes and real planes require maintenance to be operated safely. [3] _____, they both need to be fueled before they can lift off. In a way, a model airplane enthusiast serves as the ground crew for the model aircraft. He or she must refuel the model plane before each flight and do a visual check of the aircraft. The model airplane flyer must [4] _____ test the flight controls just as a real pilot checks the flight controls of his or her plane before takeoff.

3 [5] _____ similarity between the two airplanes is the physics involved in flying them. For [6] _____, just like a real airplane, a model plane is powered by a gas engine that **spins** a propeller to create forward power. A model airplane also has wings, which create lift[1]. This lift keeps the model floating in the air. [7] _____, both planes use ailerons[2] and flaps to control their direction. Surprisingly, [8] _____ a model plane is only five feet (1.5 meters) long, it flies at about 80 mph (129 kph), which is just 20 mph (32 kph) slower than a real plane.

[1]lift: the force that holds an airplane in the air
[2]aileron: a flat piece of metal attached to the back end of an airplane wing

ACTIVITY 11 | Editing for errors

Read paragraphs 4 and 5 of Essay 6.2. These paragraphs have 10 errors: article (1), parallel structure (2), subject-verb agreement (2), verb tense (2), word form (2), and fragment (1). Find and correct them.

ESSAY 6.2 (CONT.)

4   Both types of planes have similar parts as well. Both have a throttle that controls the speedy of the plane. Both are using a rudder on the vertical tail fin that steers plane left and right while in the air. In addition, real airplanes and model airplanes uses ailerons on the wings, allowing the planes to move to the left or to the right. In a real airplane, a foot pedal steered the plane left and right while in the air and guides the plane left and right while it is sitting on the ground. Similarly, a remote-controlled switch **accomplish** the same left-right **motion** on a model airplane.

5   The average person is surprisingly to find that there are so many similarities between model airplanes and flying real airplanes. Just like a real plane, a model airplane requires pre-flight procedures, how it operates on the same **principles** of physics, and has similar parts and systems. Although it is not exactly the same as the **original**. A model airplane is quite close to it. Like flying on real planes, flying model planes will likely continue to be a popular activity in the years to come.

ACTIVITY 12 | Analyzing an essay

Answer these questions about Essay 6.2, "Flying a Model Plane vs. a Real Plane"

1. What is the writer's purpose in this essay? Begin your sentence with *The purpose of . . .*

    _____

2. What are the points of comparison in this essay?

    _____

    _____

3. What method of organization does the writer use: point-by-point or block?

    _____

4. Underline the thesis statement. Is the thesis restated in the conclusion? _____
    If yes, underline that sentence (or sentences) in the conclusion.

BUILDING BETTER VOCABULARY

WORDS TO KNOW

accomplish (v)	motion (n)	resident (n) **AW**
constant (adj) **AW**	original (n)	severe (adj)
constitute (v) **AW**	paralyze (v)	spin (v)
freedom (n)	preference (n)	threat (n)
frigid (adj)	principle (n) **AW**	unbearable (adj)
humidity (n)	procedure (n) **AW**	urban (adj)
illustrate (v) **AW**	remarkably (adv)	

ACTIVITY 13 | Word associations

Circle the word or phrase that is more closely related to the bold word on the left.

1.	accomplish	fail	succeed
2.	constant	continue	stop
3.	freedom	allowed	not allowed
4.	illustrate	hide	show
5.	motion	active	not active
6.	original	first	last
7.	principle	suggestion	rule
8.	remarkably	surprising	normal
9.	severe	strong	weak
10.	threat	danger	safety

ACTIVITY 14 | Collocations

Fill in the blank with the word that most naturally completes the phrase.

constitute	paralyzed	procedure	resident	spin

1. _____ around in a circle

2. teenagers _____ a majority

3. _____ of a city

4. the company's hiring _____

5. be _____ with fear

| constant | freedom | illustrate | original | preference |

6. a(n) _____ painting

7. a strong _____ for short films

8. _____ to say what is on one's mind

9. _____ my point

10. in _____ motion

ACTIVITY 15 | Word forms

Complete each sentence with the correct word form. Use the correct form of the verbs.

NOUN	VERB	ADJECTIVE	ADVERB	SENTENCES
accomplishment	accomplish	accomplished		**1.** Thomas Edison's greatest _____ was the invention of the light bulb. **2.** Professional musicians are quite _____.
constant		constant	constantly	**3.** Successful farming often requires _____ temperatures. **4.** Tech companies are _____ creating new versions of products.
freedom	free	free	freely	**5.** There is a saying that _____ is not free. **6.** Fishermen sometimes _____ the fish they catch.

Fishermen use a net to catch fish off the back of their boat in the UK.

NOUN	VERB	ADJECTIVE	ADVERB	SENTENCES
preference	prefer	preferred / preferable	preferably	**7.** Some people _____ sweet sauces to savory ones. **8.** The students have a _____ for multiple-choice exams.
threat	threaten	threatened / threatening	threateningly	**9.** The black clouds looked _____ . **10.** Some parents _____ to take away their children's phones.

ACTIVITY 16 | Vocabulary in writing

Choose five words from Words to Know. Write a complete sentence with each word.

1. _____

2. _____

3. _____

4. _____

5. _____

BUILDING BETTER SENTENCES

ACTIVITY 17 | Editing from teacher's comments

Read the teacher comments. Then make the corrections.

PARAGRAPH 6.2

Mapping the World's Largest Caves

Scientists have begun mapping three giant cave [s/p] in China using laser scanning technology. This expedition marks the first time anyone attempts [vf] to use this technology to map underground caves. The technology is especially useful because it is difficult to see the walls and ceilings in the large caves with traditional lights. For the scientists, the highlight of the expedition seeing images [frag] of 50-meter-tall stalagmites. Stalagmites are beautiful columns that rise from the floor of the cave. Without the lasers, this would not have been possibility [wf]. Lasers can also be used for other things such as medical procedures. [Does this sentence support the topic sentence?] Laser scanning technology will help scientists to better understand caves for years to come.

Chinese villagers explore a newly-discovered cave in southwest China.

ACTIVITY 18 | Editing

Read the paragraph and notice the underlined words. If there is an error, write the correction.

PARAGRAPH 6.3

Life on Mars

It is possible that life already *exists* exist on Mars. Some scientists believe that water have existed on Mars for two or three billion years. Scientists have also discovered methane gas on Mars. On our planet Earth, microbes, single-celled life forms, is able to live on the bottom of the ocean by eat methane. Finding any live on Mars, even microbes, would be one of the bigger scientific discoveries of all time.

ACTIVITY 19 | Combining sentences

Combine the ideas into one sentence. You may change the word forms, but do not change or omit any ideas. There may be more than one answer.

1. Stars are light years away from Earth.
Stars contain a lot of heat.
The heat is extreme.

_____

_____

2. Coffee farming can be environmentally friendly.
Coffee farming can be sustainable.
Farmers can still profit from it.

_____

_____

3. There was a period of rain in Kenya.
The rain was heavy.
It exposed a big crack in the earth.
The crack measures 50 feet deep.
It measures 65 feet wide.

_____

_____

WRITING

ACTIVITY 20 | Writing a comparison essay

1. Choose a topic below or think of your own.

- Compare a sports team's (or an athlete's) previous and current performances and records.
- Compare the cuisine of one country with the cuisine of another country.
- Compare or contrast the anticipation and expectation of an important event (such as your first day of school or your first trip on an airplane) with the reality of that event.
- Compare or contrast two people that you admire.
- Compare or contrast two movies of the same type, such as science fiction or comedy.

My topic: _____

2. Brainstorm ideas about your topic on a separate piece of paper.

3. Outline your essay using a block or a point-by-point outline. Then exchange outlines with a partner. Read your partner's outline. Use the Peer Editing Form for Outlines in the *Writer's Handbook* to help you comment on your partner's outline. Use your partner's feedback to revise your outline.

4. Write the first draft of your comparison essay using your outline.

5. Read your partner's writing. Use Peer Editing Form 6 in the *Writer's Handbook* to help you comment on your partner's writing. Consider your partner's comments as you revise your work.

6. Revise your first draft. Use the comments from your partner to help you edit and revise your writing. Be sure that you use correct vocabulary, correct punctuation, and clear language. When you finish, add an appropriate title.

7. Use the checklist as you proofread the final draft.

- ☐ I have a hook to start my introduction.
- ☐ My thesis statement contains a clear controlling idea.
- ☐ I followed either the block or point-by-point method carefully.
- ☐ I used appropriate connectors and transitions for comparison/contrast.
- ☐ I used comparative and superlative forms correctly.
- ☐ Items in lists have parallel structure.
- ☐ The concluding paragraph restates the thesis and summarizes the main points.

For help with wording, see the *Useful Words and Phrases* in the *Writer's Handbook*.

Additional Topics for Writing

Here are five ideas for writing a comparison essay. Choose a topic and follow your teacher's instructions.

TOPIC 1: Look at the photo at the beginning of the unit. Write about another place with sharp contrasts. These contrasts could be environmental, social, economic, etc.

TOPIC 2: Choose one modern convenience. Compare life before this invention and life now.

TOPIC 3: Compare the skills needed for two professions.

TOPIC 4: Compare or contrast shopping at stores and shopping online.

TOPIC 5: Compare two ways to prepare for a big test.

WRITER'S NOTE How Many Paragraphs Does an Essay Have?

In some writing classes, the instructor may ask for a five-paragraph essay. The five-paragraph essay consists of a clear beginning, a body of three paragraphs, and a conclusion. However, an essay can have as few as three paragraphs and as many as ten (or more) paragraphs, as long as there is a clear beginning, a body, and a conclusion. The content of the essay, not the type of writing, determines the number of paragraphs that a particular essay has.

TEST PREP

TIP

Running out of time at the end of a writing test can seriously affect your score. Once you have written your introduction and the body paragraphs, check your remaining time. Then read through what you have written to check for the clarity of your ideas. If you are running out of time, write a very brief conclusion. Instructors are more interested in the ideas you present than in your conclusion.

You should spend about 40 minutes on this task. Write an essay about the following topic:

Compare two ways to communicate with family and friends.

For this comparison essay, use point-by-point organization. Include a short introduction (with a thesis statement), two or three body paragraphs, and a conclusion. Make sure your points of development are clear. Write at least 250 words.

7 | Problem-Solution Essays

With environmental changes, some animals in the Antarctic are facing loss of habitat, food shortages, and other problems. Biologists attach Crittercams to penguins to see first-hand how the penguins are coping with these pressures.

FREEWRITE | Look at the photo and read the caption. On a separate piece of paper, write about another problem that environmental changes create and possible solutions to that problem.

ELEMENTS OF GREAT WRITING

What Is a Problem-Solution Essay?

In a **problem-solution essay,** the writer explains a problem and offers one or more solutions.

The introductory paragraph typically:
- presents the problem
- includes background information on the problem
- explains why the problem is important or why the reader should care about it

Alternatively, the writer may divide the introduction of the problem into two paragraphs. In this case, the writer presents the problem and background information in the introductory paragraph and then explains why it is important in the first body paragraph. Either way, the writer should clearly identify the problem and explain its importance at the beginning of the essay.

The body paragraphs present one or more possible solutions. There are two approaches:
- present one solution, with two or more reasons why or how it would be effective
- present two or more solutions, with an explanation of why or how each would be effective

Finally, the concluding paragraph provides a summary of the main points. It may also offer a call to action—recommendations for what could potentially prevent similar problems from occurring in the future.

In summary, the problem-solution essay:
- identifies and explains the problem
- gives background information or the history of the problem
- explains why the problem is important
- offers one or more solutions to the problem
- summarizes the main points and may include a call to action

In a problem-solution essay, the writer often chooses a topic where there are a number of possible solutions. In this case, the writer might choose to write about the *best* solution. For instance, if the problem is too much traffic, the essay can focus on one solution: better public transportation. The body paragraphs explain how this solution would work and the reasons this solution would be effective.

On the other hand, the writer might choose to provide two or three solutions to this problem, such as better public transportation, ride-sharing, and fees for road use during peak hours. In this model, each solution would be a separate body paragraph.

ACTIVITY 1 | Identifying solutions to a problem

With a partner, read the following essay titles. Write two or three possible solutions. Then circle the best solution.

1. Title: Preventing Head Injuries in Sports

   Solutions: _creating awareness, safety equipment, a change in rules_ _____

2. Title: Bullying (or Attacking Others) on Social Media

   Solutions: _____

   _____

3. Title: Stress in College

   Solutions: _____

   _____

4. Title: Endangered Wildlife

   Solutions: _____

   _____

5. Title: Unemployment for Young Adults

   Solutions: _____

   _____

6. Title: Internet Security

   Solutions: _____

   _____

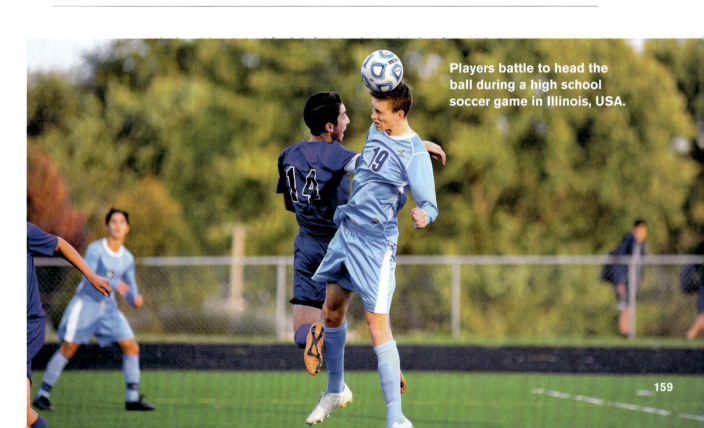

Players battle to head the ball during a high school soccer game in Illinois, USA.

Grammar: Adverb Clauses

An **adverb clause** is a dependent clause that is connected to an independent clause. Like all clauses, it has a subject and a verb. An adverb clause functions like an adverb. It gives information such as when, why, how, how much, and under what conditions the action in the main clause takes place.

Adverb clauses begin with a subordinating conjunction such as *when*, *because*, or *if*. **Subordinating conjunctions** show the relationship between the ideas in the adverb clause and in the main clause.

Note that an adverb clause can come before or after the main (independent) clause. If it comes before, it is followed by a comma.

Study the list of common subordinating conjunctions categorized by function and the example sentences with adverb clauses.

SUBORDINATING CONJUNCTIONS	SENTENCES WITH ADVERB CLAUSES
TIME	
after as soon as before once since until when while	<u>**After**</u> **the hurricane hit our town**, the streets were flooded. Some people check their phones **as soon as they wake up.** <u>**Since**</u> **the company started its new marketing strategy**, sales have increased significantly. The candidates waited nervously **while the votes were being counted.**
REASON	
because since as	<u>**Because**</u> **the election was close**, the candidate asked for a recount. Coastal cities are in danger **since sea levels are rising.**
CONDITION	
if unless even if	<u>**If**</u> **the stock market goes down**, investors get nervous. Drivers pay more to rent cars **unless they are at least 25 years old.**
PURPOSE	
so so that	Some students study hard on weekdays **so that they can relax on weekends.**
HOW/MANNER	
as if as though	The man walked **as if he had an injury.** It looks **as though it will rain.**
CONCESSION/CONTRAST	
although even though whereas while	Poachers still hunt elephants for their ivory **although it is against the law.** <u>**While**</u> **traveling alone can be stressful**, it also pushes people to be more outgoing.

ACTIVITY 2 | Using subordinating conjunctions

Read the sentences. Circle the correct subordinating conjunction.

1. Teenagers often feel (as though / although) they are alone.

2. Sea levels will continue to rise (while / unless) climate change is slowed down.

3. (Because / Before) children do not get enough exercise, they are becoming unhealthier.

4. (Once / Since) unemployment has increased in the past year, consumer spending has dropped significantly.

5. (When / Even if) athletes train too hard, they often sustain injuries.

6. One should always prepare for a job interview (so that / as if) it can go as smoothly as possible.

7. (Although / Unless) the Internet allows people to get information quickly, the information is not always reliable.

8. People sometimes continue bad habits (if / even though) these habits have a negative effect on their lives.

ACTIVITY 3 | Identifying adverb clauses and main clauses

Go back to Activity 2. Underline the adverb clause in each sentence.

An elephant with large tusks in Addo Elephant National Park in South Africa

ACTIVITY 4 | Expanding a paragraph into an essay

Paragraph 7.1 has been expanded into Essay 7.1. Connect similar sections of the paragraph and essay using lines or different-colored highlighters. The topic sentence and thesis statement have both been highlighted in green. Then answer the questions that follow.

WORDS TO KNOW Paragraph 7.1 and Essay 7.1

aspect: (n) a feature, part of
come across: (v phr) to give the appearance of
content: (n) the ideas or meanings expressed in a speech or piece of writing
deliver: (v) to give
element: (n) a part or aspect
focus: (v) to center one's attention on

overcome: (v) to fight against successfully
slight: (adj) small
sufficient: (adj) adequate, enough
survey: (n) questions designed to measure the opinions of a group of people
task: (n) an assignment; a job to be performed
terrifying: (adj) causing strong fear, frightening

PARAGRAPH 7.1

A Fear Worse than Death

According to several recent **surveys**, some people fear public speaking more than they do death. Fortunately, this fear can be **overcome** with two simple methods: practice and using positive energy from the audience. Practicing for a speech is essential. After the **task** of writing the speech is complete, speakers must practice, practice, practice. The more times they rehearse the speech, the more comfortable they are discussing the topic. Using aids such as mirrors or video recordings as they practice can show speakers what they look and sound like to the audience. Video is particularly helpful as it can be watched many times, with the presenters **focusing** on one **element** at a time. Another remedy for public speaking fears is using the audience's positive energy. Speakers need to remember that the audience wants them to succeed. Something as basic as a small nod or a smile from a member of the audience should give courage and confidence to the presenters behind the podium. While it is easy for nervous speakers to focus only on getting through the presentation, using the audience's good will goes a long way in making a speech better. All in all, these two strategies are sure to help with fear of public speaking. With proper practice and audience empathy[1], it is possible to overcome the fear of public speaking and **deliver** a successful speech.

[1]empathy: the ability to understand the feelings of another person

A Fear Worse than Death

1   According to several recent **surveys**, the biggest fear for most people is the fear of making a speech in public. More than a fear of spiders or death, public speaking is something that often causes people to break out into a cold sweat, start shaking uncontrollably, and even feel as though they are about to die. Many jobs, classes, and social events require a person to be able to **deliver** a good public speech. Fortunately, the fear of public speaking can be **overcome** with two simple methods: practice and using positive energy from the audience.

2   **Sufficient** practice of a speech is the first key to overcoming this fear. Most people are amazed at how comfortable they are giving a public speech once they have properly prepared and practiced. Practicing a speech numerous times reduces the fear of **coming across** as unprepared. Some speakers stand in front of a mirror to practice their speech, but others prefer to have a video recording made, either by a friend or colleague. The benefits of this type of visual practice are many. Speakers can watch the video again and again, **focusing** on a different **aspect** of the speech each time. **Elements** such as speed, body language, **content**, and other areas of concern can get the attention that they need. The result of sufficient practice is a more confident speaker and a more effective speech.

3   The second key to overcoming the fear of public speaking is to use positive energy from the audience. Speakers need to remember a very important thing: no one wants to see them fail in front of a group. The audience members have probably given speeches themselves, so they know how **terrifying** it can be. In addition, a poorly given speech is not only uncomfortable for the speaker, but it is also uncomfortable for the audience. They want to see the speaker succeed because it is a more enjoyable experience for everyone involved. Speakers can look at the faces of the audience and search for that small nod of agreement or the **slight** smile, which is often enough to make even the most fearful speakers relax. People sometimes forget that speech-giving is actually a two-way street. By giving and receiving positive thoughts and energy, both the speaker and the audience will have a positive experience.

4   There is no question that public speaking can be frightening. However, there is also no question that it is an extremely valuable skill to have. Whether giving the commencement speech at a graduation or a simple toast at a wedding, with proper practice and audience empathy, it is possible to overcome the fear of public speaking and deliver a successful speech.

A panel of speakers at a conference in Canada

1. What is the purpose of this essay? Begin your sentence with *The purpose of . . .*

_____

2. Does the writer use a one-solution or a multiple-solution approach?

_____

3. Underline the writer's hook. Is it a description, a quote, a fact, or an interesting idea?

_____

4. Where is the thesis restated in the essay? _____

5. In the introductory paragraph, what details does the writer give to show that fear of public

speaking is an important problem to solve? _____

_____

6. What solutions are presented in the body paragraphs? _____

_____

7. What does the writer do in the conclusion? _____

_____

Organizing a Problem-Solution Essay

There are two ways to organize a problem-solution essay: presenting one solution or presenting more than one solution.

Introduction	• Identify the problem • Provide background information • Explain why the problem is important • State the thesis, which introduces the solution(s)	
	ONE SOLUTION	**MORE THAN ONE SOLUTION**
Body	**Body Paragraph 1:** Present the solution, explaining one reason why it would be effective **Body Paragraph 2:** Explain a second reason why the solution would be effective (**Body Paragraph 3:** Explain a third reason why the solution would be effective)	**Body Paragraph 1:** Present the first solution, explaining why it would be effective **Body Paragraph 2:** Present a second solution, explaining why it would be effective (**Body Paragraph 3:** Present a third solution, explaining why it would be effective)
Conclusion	• Restate the thesis • Summarize the main points • Issue a call to action if appopriate	

ACTIVITY 5 | Outlining a problem-solution essay

Complete the outline for an essay on the problem of homesickness with words and phrases from the box.

action	friendships	no time	reach out	stay busy
communication	hook	people	sad	support

I. Introduction

    A. _____ : Surveys report that almost 70 percent of students attending university for the first time feel homesick.

    B. Describe problem, background information, why it is important

    C. Thesis statement: Two strategies are helpful in overcoming homesickness.

II. Body Paragraph 1: Get involved

    A. _____

        1. Get involved in new activities

        2. Leave _____ to feel sad

    B. Meet _____

        1. Have less time alone

        2. Develop new _____

III. Body Paragraph 2: Plan _____ with family and friends

    A. _____

        1. Schedule time to talk with parents

        2. Text with friends

    B. Talk about personal feelings

        1. Share _____ emotions with others

        2. Get their _____

IV. Conclusion

    A. Restate the thesis

    B. Call to _____

SUPPORT (vertical label beside II)

SUPPORT (vertical label beside III)

Grammar: Sentence Types

There are three basic types of sentences in English: **simple**, **compound**, and **complex**. These labels indicate how the information in a sentence is organized, not how difficult the content is.

SENTENCE TYPE	EXAMPLES
Simple	**One independent clause (subject + verb)** S V <u>People</u> in their 20s <u>prefer</u> to live in cities for several reasons. S V Too much <u>sitting</u> <u>is</u> bad for your back. S V The <u>electricity</u> <u>went off</u> in the storm.
Compound	**Independent clause, coordinating conjunction + independent clause** S V conj S Many Arctic <u>animals</u> <u>are</u> white to blend in with the snow, **but** this <u>snow</u> V <u>has been melting</u> in many areas. S V conj S V The <u>lack</u> of rain <u>killed</u> the crops, **so** the <u>farmer</u> <u>lost</u> money.
Complex	**Independent-dependent clause combination** S adj clause V <u>People</u> **who are naturally outgoing** often <u>prefer</u> to wake up late. adv clause S V **Although students read a lot of material online**, <u>they</u> <u>do not remember</u> it well much of the time. S V adv clause <u>Monkeys</u> in Japan <u>take</u> baths in hot springs **because the heat lowers stress**.

Macaque monkeys bathe in hot springs in Nagano, Japan.

Arctic polar bears moving through pack ice in the Svalbard archipelago in Norway

ACTIVITY 6 | Identifying sentence types

Identify the following sentences from Paragraph 7.1 and Essay 7.1 as simple (*S*), compound (*C*), or complex (*CX*).

_____ **1.** Practicing for a speech is essential.

_____ **2.** After the task of writing the speech is complete, speakers must practice, practice, practice.

_____ **3.** Something as basic as a small nod or a smile from a member of the audience should give courage and confidence to the presenters behind the podium.

_____ **4.** While it is easy for nervous speakers to focus only on getting through the presentation, using the audience's good will goes a long way in making a speech better.

_____ **5.** More than a fear of spiders or death, public speaking is something that often causes people to break out into a cold sweat, start shaking uncontrollably, and even feel as though they are about to die.

_____ **6.** Sufficient practice of a speech is the first key to overcoming this fear.

_____ **7.** Practicing a speech numerous times reduces the fear of coming across as unprepared.

_____ **8.** Some speakers stand in front of a mirror to practice their speech, but others prefer to have a video recording made, either by a friend or colleague.

_____ **9.** The audience members have probably given speeches themselves, so they know how terrifying it can be.

_____ **10.** They want to see the speaker succeed because it is a more enjoyable experience for everyone involved.

The Rio Celeste Waterfall in Terino Volcano National Park in Costa Rica

Sentence Variety

Sentence variety makes writing more interesting and creates a rhythm. When sentences in a paragraph are of similar length or follow a similar pattern (for example, S + V + O), they can be hard to read. Read the paragraphs below. Which one uses greater sentence variety?

a.   Costa Rica is a beautiful country. It has a variety of microclimates. It is hot and humid at the beaches. However, it is cool and damp in the mountains. There are cloud forests. There are also tropical rain forests. The weather near the volcanoes is often different from the weather on the coast.

b.   The beautiful country of Costa Rica has a variety of microclimates. While the beaches are often very hot and humid, the mountains may be cool and damp. The cloud forests, which are higher and therefore cooler, differ greatly from the warm, wet tropical rain forests. When Costa Ricans on the coast are wearing shorts and sandals, their counterparts near the volcanoes may have on jackets and boots. Costa Rica is a small country of many climates!

Notice that the second paragraph is more interesting because it uses greater sentence variety. As you write, look for places to use different types of sentences.

ACTIVITY 7 | Using sentence variety

On a separate piece of paper, rewrite Paragraph 7.2 with greater sentence variety.

PARAGRAPH 7.2

Preventing Head Injuries in Sports

Many sports involve physical contact. These sports include football, hockey, soccer, and rugby. Kids play these sports. They often hit their heads and get concussions. Too many concussions cause brain damage. There are two solutions to this problem. First, sporting authorities can change their rules. The new rules should reduce physical contact. For example, a rule could forbid tackling. Second, athletes can use better safety equipment. For example, rugby players could be required to wear headgear.

ACTIVITY 8 | Analyzing an essay

Read the essay and answer the questions that follow. Note: The essay does not have a conclusion. You will write one in the next activity.

> **WORDS TO KNOW** Essay 7.2
>
> **barrier:** (n) something that blocks the way
> **distraction:** (n) something that prevents someone from giving full attention
> **diverse:** (adj) varied; different from each other
> **exposure:** (n) contact with
> **ill-equipped:** (adj) badly prepared
>
> **obligation:** (n) a requirement to do something
> **prioritize:** (v) to put in order of importance
> **put off:** (v phr) to postpone, delay
> **retention:** (n) the ability to keep or remember something

ESSAY 7.2

Smart Time Management: The Key to Success

1   It is no secret that many students lead busy, **diverse** lives. Between school, work, family **obligations**, and a social life, there can be a lot to juggle[1]. Add to this an increased **exposure** to technology, and the **distractions** may feel almost insurmountable[2]. Students in particular struggle because they are **ill-equipped** to handle their time wisely. This can have a negative impact on everything from grades to happiness and even health. Poor time management can be a real **barrier** to success. Fortunately, there are two simple strategies students can use to solve this problem: planning ahead and limiting distractions.

2   Students can be more successful by simply planning their study schedule. For example, many students **put off** studying for a test until the last minute. However, it is much less stressful and much more effective to break up study time over the course of several days. Instead of studying for five hours the day before a big exam, or "cramming," students can plan ahead and study for two hours per night the three nights before the exam. This "timed study" not only decreases stress, it also leads to better long-term **retention** of the material. Students should also plan their week out in advance, budgeting time each day for classes, study, self-care, and other responsibilities. They should also **prioritize** their tasks, doing the most important ones first. Students who begin each week with a clear plan tend to achieve greater success than those who do not.

3   Another way students can better manage their time is to understand the distractions they face and limit them. The average student spends more than six hours a week on social media. Even more traditional media can be a distraction as the average adult watches more than five hours of television each day. As a solution, by limiting TV to one hour per day, 28 extra hours become available each week, which is more than enough time to accomplish important tasks. Students who stay away from their social media accounts in the morning are able to start their day with some exercise and a quick study session instead. They save distractions for after they have completed their tasks. The key to success here is not to completely remove distractions, but to simply limit them.

[1]juggle: to handle several tasks at the same time
[2]insurmountable: extremely difficult; nearly impossible

A high school student's attention is divided between class and text messages.

1. What is the purpose of this essay? Begin your sentence with *The purpose of . . .*

_____

_____

2. According to the essay, why is time management a significant problem for students?

_____

_____

3. What two solutions does the writer suggest?

_____

_____

4. What support is given for the first solution?

_____

_____

5. What support is given for the second solution?

_____

_____

6. Which solution is more persuasive? Explain your answer.

_____

_____

ACTIVITY 9 | Writing a conclusion with sentence variety

Use these simple sentences to write a conclusion for the essay. Follow the steps below to create greater sentence variety. Delete and add extra words as needed.

    a. Every day, the number of distractions is increasing.

    b. Every day, the amount of time is decreasing.

    c. It seems that way, at least.

    d. Social media has greatly enriched people's lives.

    e. There is no question about this.

    f. Students can spend too much time on distractions.

    g. When this happens, accomplishing tasks becomes more difficult.

    h. This is especially true for students.

    i. Time is a limited resource.

    j. Students need to realize this.

    k. Students need to plan their time wisely.

    l. Poor time management prevents students from being successful.

    m. The success is in school and their lives.

    n. Luckily, this barrier can be overcome rather easily.

    o. To do this, follow these simple recommendations.

1. Combine sentences a–c. Begin with *It seems that . . .*

2. Combine sentences d and e. Begin with *There is no question that . . .*

3. Combine sentences f–h. Use an adverbial clause of time.

4. Combine sentences i–k. Use a transition word or phrase.

5. Combine sentences l and m. Use a transition word or phrase.

6. Combine sentences n and o.

BUILDING BETTER VOCABULARY

WORDS TO KNOW

aspect (n) AW	element (n) AW	put off (v phr)
barrier (n)	exposure (n) AW	retention (n) AW
come across (v phr)	focus (v) AW	slight (adj)
content (n)	ill-equipped (adj)	sufficient (adj) AW
deliver (v)	obligation (n)	survey (n) AW
distraction (n)	overcome (v)	task (n) AW
diverse (adj) AW	prioritize (v) AW	terrifying (adj)

ACTIVITY 10 | Word associations

Circle the word that is more closely related to the bold word or phrase on the left.

1. come across	appear	describe
2. content	audience	subject
3. deliver	take	give
4. element	part	whole
5. focus	attention	confusion
6. obligation	responsibility	need
7. retention	lose	keep
8. slight	big	small
9. survey	lists	questions
10. task	job	game

ACTIVITY 11 | Collocations

Fill in the blank with the word that most naturally completes the phrase.

barriers	deliver	ill-equipped	overcome	prioritize

1. _____ important tasks

2. _____ a speech to an audience

3. _____ to handle the problem

4. _____ difficult challenges

5. _____ to success

aspects	distraction	exposure	obligations	surveys

6. take online _____

7. discuss many _____ of the issue

8. a(n) _____ from work

9. limit _____ to the sun

10. have family _____

ACTIVITY 12 | Word forms

Complete each sentence with the correct word form. Use the correct form of the verbs.

NOUN	VERB	ADJECTIVE	ADVERB	SENTENCES
delivery	deliver	deliverable		**1.** There is no mail _____ on Sundays. **2.** Many grocery stores will now _____ food to your home.
diversity	diversify	diverse		**3.** The company is hoping to _____ its sales force. **4.** There is a lack of _____ in the student body.
exposure	expose	expository / exposed		**5.** It is a good idea to protect oneself from too much sun _____ . **6.** Parents should _____ their children to a variety of foods.
obligation	obligate	obligatory		**7.** I think that citizens have an _____ to vote. **8.** In some countries, military service is _____ .
terror	terrify	terrifying / terrified	terrifyingly	**9.** The idea of speaking in public fills many people with _____ . **10.** High places _____ certain people.

ACTIVITY 13 | Vocabulary in writing

Choose five words from Words to Know. Write a complete sentence with each word.

1. _____

2. _____

3. _____

4. _____

5. _____

BUILDING BETTER SENTENCES

ACTIVITY 14 | Editing from teacher's comments

Read the teacher comments. Then make the corrections.

PARAGRAPH 7.3

The Problem with Bright Nights

   The night skies are so bright in the United States that most people under the age of 40 <u>has</u> never   *s/v agr*
experienced true darkness. Astronomers have <u>the</u> scale for rating darkness, with 1 being the darkest   *art*
and 9 the brightest. Because of light pollution, most people live in levels 5 through 8. Not only does
too much light at night waste electricity, it can also cause sleep <u>problem</u>, obesity, and even cancer. One   *s/p*
solution to this problem <u>will be</u> to use motion detectors to turn the lights on and off around the home.   *vf*
These lights come on when people leave or enter a <u>home. But</u> the lights turn off after a few minutes.   *punct*
This automatic system saves money and <u>electric</u>, and it will also reduce the amount of light that pollutes   *wf*
neighborhoods around the United States. <u>If we each do our part to limit the use of light at night.</u> The   *frag*
beautiful night sky will be appreciated by a greater number of people, especially in urban areas.

WRITER'S NOTE Adding Sentence Variety

Remember to look for places to add sentence variety in your writing. You can do this by using simple, compound, and complex sentences. You can also add variety by starting a sentence with a prepositional phrase instead of starting with a subject.

Students have a lot to manage between studying, family obligations, social life, and sometimes work.

Between school, family obligations, social life, and sometimes work, students have a lot to manage.

ACTIVITY 15 | Combining sentences

Combine the ideas into one sentence. You may change the word forms, but do not change or omit any ideas. There may be more than one answer.

1. Languages die with their last speaker.
Every two weeks a language dies.
Fifty to ninety percent will disappear.
This will happen by the next century.

_____

_____

2. The meat substitute is tasty.
The meat substitute is made from soy.
The meat substitute is made from peas.
Some consumers may not taste the difference.

_____

_____

3. Coral reefs are in danger.
One reason is development.
In Jordan, some coral reefs were moved.
These coral reefs are doing well.

_____

_____

Light pollution in Lombardy, Italy

Volunteers packing food at a food bank. Food banks provide free food to those in need.

ACTIVITY 16 | Writing about a photo

On a separate piece of paper, write a short paragraph of five to eight sentences about the photo. Focus on one or two solutions to the problem. Make sure that you use a variety of sentence types.

WRITING

ACTIVITY 17 | Writing a problem-solution essay

Follow these steps for your problem-solution essay.

1. Choose a topic below or think of your own.
   - Addiction to soft drinks
   - Stress
   - Disagreement with a friend
   - Poor sleep

2. Brainstorm ideas about your topic on a separate piece of paper.

3. Outline your essay. Then exchange outlines with a partner. Read your partner's outline. Use the Peer Editing Form for Outlines in the *Writer's Handbook* to help you comment on your partner's outline. Use your partner's feedback to revise your outline.

4. Write the first draft of your problem-solution essay, using your outline.

5. Exchange papers with a partner. Read your partner's writing. Then use Peer Editing Form 7 in the *Writer's Handbook* to help you comment on your partner's writing.

6. Revise your first draft using the comments from your partner to help you.

7. Proofread the final draft. Use the checklist as well as the feedback you received. In addition, try reading your essay aloud. When you finish, add a title to your essay.

☐ I provided necessary background information and explained the significance of the problem.
☐ I followed either the one-solution or multiple-solution method.
☐ I explained why the solution(s) would be effective.
☐ I used adverb clauses correctly.
☐ My writing contains a variety of sentence types.
☐ The concluding paragraph restates the thesis and summarizes the main points.

For help with phrasing, see *Useful Words and Phrases* in the *Writer's Handbook*.

Additional Topics for Writing

Here are five ideas for writing a problem-solution essay. Choose a topic and follow your teacher's instructions.

TOPIC 1:   Describe a relationship problem at home, work, or school and offer a solution.

TOPIC 2:   Choose one problem in your city or neighborhood and suggest a solution.

TOPIC 3:   Describe a problem caused by climate change and propose a solution.

TOPIC 4:   Choose a problem that university students face and suggest two solutions.

TOPIC 5:   Write about two solutions for reducing debt.

TEST PREP

> **TIP**
> Writing a four-paragraph essay in only 40 minutes can be stressful, but it is worth the time and effort to write a quick outline before you begin the essay. This will help you stay focused on your thesis statement and supporting ideas. Make sure to include as many supporting details as you can in your outline. This will save time when you are ready to write.

You should spend about 40 minutes on this task. Write a four-paragraph essay about the following topic:

Protecting personal information on the Internet

For this problem-solution essay, suggest two solutions. Include a short introduction explaining the problem. Each body paragraph should offer a different solution. Include details and examples to support your solutions. Write at least 250 words.

WRITER'S HANDBOOK

UNDERSTANDING THE WRITING PROCESS

Writing is a process. Writers rarely write an essay from introduction to conclusion in one sitting. Instead, they follow certain steps. Use these steps as a guideline when you write. The writing process is not always linear. You may return to earlier steps as needed.

Step 1:   Choose a Topic

Step 2:   Brainstorm

Step 3:   Outline

Step 4:   Write the First Draft

Step 5:   Get Feedback from a Peer

Step 6:   Reread, Rethink, Rewrite

Step 7:   Proofread the Final Draft

Steps in the Writing Process

Step 1: Choose a Topic

Sometimes you will be asked to write an essay on a broad topic such as *An Influential Person*. In this case, you can choose any person you want as long as you can clearly show how that person has influenced you or others. You should try to choose a topic that you are interested in.

To walk through the steps in the writing process, consider the given assignment: "Write an essay in which you discuss one aspect of being a vegetarian." As you consider the assignment, think about what kind of essay you want to write such as:
- A classification of the types of vegetarian diets
- A historical account of vegetarianism
- An argument that being a vegetarian is better than eating meat

The type of essay you write (argument, comparison, etc.) will depend on the topic you choose (or are given), and the ideas you decide to develop.

Step 2: Brainstorm

Write every idea about your topic that comes to mind. Some of these ideas will be better than others; write them all. The main purpose of brainstorming is to write as many ideas as possible. If one idea looks promising, circle it or put a check next to it. If you write an idea that you know right away you are not going to use, cross it out.

Brainstorming methods include making lists, clustering similar ideas, or diagramming. Here is an example of a student's brainstorming diagram on the topic of "being a vegetarian."

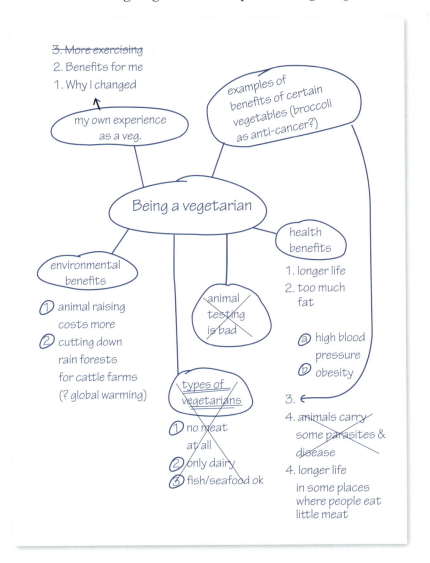

As you can see, the student considered many aspects of being a vegetarian. As she organized her ideas, she wrote "examples of benefits of certain vegetables" as one piece of supporting information. Then she realized that this point would be good in the list of health benefits, so she drew an arrow to show that she should move it there. Since one of her brainstorming ideas (types of vegetarians) lacked supporting details and was not related to her other notes, she crossed it out.

How can you get information for this brainstorming exercise?
- You might search online for an article about vegetarianism.
- You could write a short questionnaire to give to classmates asking them about their personal knowledge of vegetarian practices.
- You could interview an expert on the topic, such as a nutritionist.

Note that any information you get from an outside source needs to be credited in your essay. As you get information, keep notes on your sources. See "Avoiding Plagiarism" in this *Writer's Handbook* for more information on citing outside sources and referencing.

Step 3: Outline

Next, you should write an outline for your essay. Here is an initial outline based on the brainstorming notes.

I. Introduction
 A. Hook
 B. Connecting information
 C. Thesis statement

II. Environmental benefits
 A. Rainforests
 B. Global warming

III. Health benefits
 A. Too much fat from meat → obesity → diseases
 B. High blood pressure and heart disease
 C. Cancer-fighting properties of broccoli and cauliflower, etc.

IV. Longer life
 A. Bad fats → cancer
 B. People in some countries live longer

V. Conclusion
 A. Restate thesis
 B. Opinion

Supporting Details

After you have chosen the main points for your essay, you need to develop some supporting details. You should include examples, reasons, explanations, definitions, or personal experiences.

One common technique for generating supporting details is to ask information questions about the topic: *Who? What? When? Where? Why? How?*

SUPPORT

What benefits does eating vegetables have?

How much longer do vegetarians live?

Why is eating meat a problem?

Step 4: Write the First Draft

In this step, you use information from your brainstorming and outline to draft the essay. When you write your first draft, pay attention to the language you use. Use a variety of sentence types. Consider your choice of vocabulary. Include specific terminology when possible, and avoid using informal or conversational language.

This first draft may contain errors, such as misspellings, incomplete ideas, and punctuation errors. At this point, you should not worry about correcting the errors. The focus should be on putting your ideas into sentences.

As you write the first draft, you may want to add information or take some out. In some cases, your first draft may not follow your outline exactly. That is OK. Writers do not always stick with their original plan or follow the steps in the writing process in order. Sometimes they go back and forth between steps. The writing process is much more like a cycle than a line.

Step 5: Get Feedback from a Peer

Peer editing is important in the writing process. You do not always see your own mistakes or places where information is missing because you are too close to the paragraph or essay that you wrote. Ask someone to read your draft and give you feedback about your writing. Choose someone that you trust and feel comfortable with. While some people feel uneasy about peer editing, the result is almost always a better essay. You can use the *Peer Editing Forms* in this *Writer's Handbook* as tools to help your peer editors. Your teacher may also give you feedback on your first draft. As you revise, consider all comments carefully.

Step 6: Reread, Rethink, Rewrite

This step consists of three parts:

1. Reread your essay and any comments from your peers or teacher.
2. Rethink your writing and address the comments.
3. Rewrite the essay.

Step 7: Proofread the Final Draft

Proofreading is the final step. It means reading for grammar, punctuation, and spelling errors and to see if the sentences flow smoothly. One good way to proofread your paper is to set it aside for several hours or a day or two. The next time you read it, your head will be clearer and you will be more likely to see any problems.

On the next two pages is a first draft of the essay on being a vegetarian. It includes comments from the teacher.

Reasons to Be a Vegetarian

1 Do you like burgers? Who doesn't? Eating meat, especially beef, is an

wrong transition?   *word choice*

important part of daily life around the world. <u>In addition</u>, this <u>high eating</u>

word choice   *word choice*

of meat is a major contributing <u>thing</u> that <u>makes</u> many deaths, including

deaths from heart-related problems. Vegetarianism has caught on slowly

transition?

in some parts of the world.^Vegetarianism is a way of life that can help

improve not only the quality of lives but also people's longevity.

Be sure your thesis matches your main points. Body par 1 seems to be about environmental impact. Also, you start with burgers but never mention them again. In general, check your transitions and word choice.

2 Because demand for meat is so high, cattle are being raised in areas

where the rainforest once stood. [As rain forest land is cleared in order to

frag

make room for the cattle ranches.] The environmental balance is being

upset. This could have serious consequences for us in both the near and long

term. How much of the current global warming is due to man's disturbing

the rain forest?

You need a topic sentence with your first supporting idea: the first reason to be a vegetarian. And add a concluding sentence that restates your main idea.

3 Meat contains a high amount of fat. Eating this fat has been connected

in research with certain kinds of cancer. Furthermore, eating animal fat can

what does 'this' refer to?

lead to obesity, and obesity can cause different kinds of disease. <u>This</u> results

in high blood pressure. Meat is high in cholesterol, and this adds to the

health problems. With the high consumption of animal fat, it is no wonder

that heart disease is a leading killer.

Try a more specific topic sentence relating to health and your thesis.

4   On the other hand, eating a vegetarian diet can improve a person's

necessary?

health. And vegetables taste good. In fact, it can even save lives. Eating

certain kinds of vegetables such as broccoli, brussel sprouts, and cauliflower,

SVA

have been shown to reduce the chance of colon cancer. Vegetables do not

contain the "bad" fats that meat does. Vegetables do not contain cholesterol

either. People with vegetarian diets live longer lives.

5   Although numerous studies have shown the benefits of vegetarianism

for people in general, I know how my life has improved since I decided to

give up meat. In 2010 I saw a show that discussed the problems connected

to animals raised for food. After I saw this show, I decided to try life without

meat. Although it was difficult at first, I have never regretted my decision.

I feel better than before and people tell me I look good. Being a vegetarian

has many benefits. Try it.

Good, clear topic sentence. Look for places to combine short sentences.

This is a good first draft. I can see that you have thought about the topic as you give some interesting reasons for being a vegetarian. To stay focused on your key points, revisit your thesis and topic sentences to be sure they clearly state the main ideas. Make sure the topic sentences support your thesis. Also, consider making a recommendation in your conclusion.

The following is an example of a completed peer editing form.

Sample Peer Editing Form

Reader: _Ali_   Date: _2/14_

1. What is the purpose of the essay? _The purpose is to explain why it's good to be a vegetarian._

2. Does the introduction have an effective hook? ☐ Yes   ☑ No

   Write it and/or suggest another one: _Do you like burgers? This sounds a little informal to me._

3. Is the thesis statement clear? ☑ Yes   ☐ No

   If yes, what is it? _Vegetarianism is a way of life that can help improve not only the quality of lives but also people's longevity._

4. Does each body paragraph have a topic sentence related to the thesis? ☐ Yes   ☑ No

   If no explain. _I think the third topic sentence is good, but the first two are not clearly related to the thesis._

5. Does the essay have a logical conclusion? ☑ Yes   ☐ No

   If yes, write it here. _Being a vegetarian has many benefits. Try it._

   If not, explain. _____

6. What do you like best about this essay? _I never thought about the environmental impact of raising cattle for us to eat. This was interesting to me._

Now read the final essay this student turned in to her teacher.

Reasons to Be a Vegetarian

1   Eating meat, especially beef, is an integral part of many cultures. Studies show, however, that the consumption of large quantities of meat is a major contributing factor toward a great many deaths, including the unnecessarily high number of deaths from heart-related problems. Although it is not widely adopted in many countries, vegetarianism is a way of life that can have a positive impact on the environment and people's health.

2   Surprising as it may sound, vegetarianism can have beneficial effects on the environment. Because demand for meat animals is so high, cattle are being raised in areas where rain forests once stood. Rain forests have been cleared to make room for cattle ranches, upsetting the environmental balance. One important impact of this kind of deforestation is increased temperatures, which contribute to global warming. If people consumed less meat, the need to clear land for cattle would decrease, helping to restore the ecological balance.

3   More important at an individual level is the question of how eating meat affects a person's health. Meat, unlike vegetables, can contain large amounts of fat. Eating this fat has been connected—in some studies —to certain kinds of cancer. If people cut down on the amount of meat they ate, they would automatically be lowering their risk of disease. Furthermore, eating animal fat can lead to obesity, which can cause numerous health problems. For example, obesity can cause people to become physically inactive and their hearts have to work harder. This results in high blood pressure. Meat is also high in cholesterol, and this only adds to health problems. Eliminating meat from their diet and eating vegetarian food would help people reduce their risk of certain diseases.

4   If people followed vegetarian diets, they would not only be healthier, but also live longer. Eating certain kinds of vegetables, such as broccoli, brussels sprouts, and cauliflower, has been shown to reduce the chance of contracting colon cancer later in life. Vegetables do not contain the "bad" fats that meat does. Vegetables do not contain cholesterol, either. Furthermore, native inhabitants of areas of the world where people eat more vegetables than meat, notably certain areas of Central Asia, routinely live to be over one hundred.

5   Numerous scientific studies have shown the benefits of vegetarianism for people in general. There is a common thread for those people who switch from eating meat to consuming only vegetable products. Although the change of diet is difficult at first, most people never regret their decision to become a vegetarian. As more and more people are becoming aware of the risks associated with meat consumption, they too will make the change.

PUNCTUATION

Capitalization

1. **Always capitalize the first word of a sentence.**
   Several factors contributed to the failure of the plan.
   Because of the weather, all flights were delayed.

2. **Always capitalize the word *I* no matter where it is in a sentence.**
   John brought the dessert, and **I** brought some drinks.
   Of all the trips that I have taken, **I** will always remember my trip to Kenya.

3. **Capitalize proper nouns—the names of specific people, places, or things. Capitalize a person's title, including *Mr., Mrs., Ms.,* and *Dr.***
   The **S**tatue of **L**iberty is located on **L**iberty **I**sland in **N**ew **Y**ork.
   Simón **B**olívar was born in **C**aracas, **V**enezuela, in **J**uly 1783.

4. **Capitalize names of countries and other geographic areas. Capitalize the names of people from those areas. Capitalize the names of languages.**
   People from **B**razil are called **B**razilians. They speak **P**ortuguese.
   There are few differences between **A**merican and **B**ritish **E**nglish.

5. **Capitalize titles of works, such as books, movies, and pieces of art.**
   *A **S**ea without **L**ife*   ***T**he **W**eather in **C**hicago and **M**iami*

   The rules for capitalizing titles are:
   • Always capitalize the first letter of a title.
   • Capitalize all content words (words that have meaning).
   • Do not capitalize function words, such as *a, an, and, the, in, with, on, for, to, above, an,* and *or.*

Commas

The comma has different functions. Here are some of the most common:

1. **A comma separates a list of three or more things.**
   She speaks French, English, and Chinese.
   He speaks French and English. (No comma is needed because there are only two items.)

2. **A comma separates two sentences connected by a coordinating conjunction (a combining word) such as *and, but, or, so, for, nor,* and *yet.***
   Six people took the course, but only five of them passed the test.
   Students can register for classes in person, or they can register by email.

3. **A comma is used to separate an introductory word or phrase from the rest of the sentence.**
   In conclusion, doctors are advising people to take more vitamins.
   Because of the heavy rains, many of the roads were flooded.

4. A comma is used to separate an appositive from the rest of the sentence. An appositive is a word or group of words that renames a noun.

subject (noun)   appositive   verb

Washington, the first president of the United States, was a clever military leader.

5. A comma is used with non-restrictive or unnecessary adjective clauses. We use a comma when the information in the clause is unnecessary or extra.

The History of Korea, <u>which is on the teacher's desk,</u> is the main book for this class.

(The name of the book is given, so the information in the adjective clause is not necessary to help the reader identify the book.)

The book <u>that is on the teacher's desk</u> is the main book for this class.

(The information in the adjective clause is necessary to identify which book. In this case, do not set off the adjective clause with a comma.)

Professor Jones, <u>who studied in Asia,</u> teaches this class.

(The name of the person is given, so the information in the adjective clause is not necessary. Commas are used.)

A professor <u>who studied in Asia</u> teaches this class.

(The information in the adjective clause is necessary to identify which professor. No commas are used.)

Apostrophes

Apostrophes have two basic uses in English. They indicate either a contraction or a possession. Note that contractions are seldom used in academic writing.

Contractions: Use an apostrophe in a contraction in place of the letter or letters that have been deleted.

        he's (he is *or* he has), they're (they are), I've (I have), we'd (we would *or* we had)

Possession: Add an apostrophe and the letter *s* after the word. If a plural word already ends in *s,* then just add an apostrophe.

        Ghandi's role in the history of India
        yesterday's paper
        the boy's books (One boy has some books.)
        the boys' books (Several boys have one or more books.)

Quotation Marks

Here are three of the most common uses for quotation marks.

1. **To mark the exact words that were spoken by someone:**
   The king said, "I refuse to give up my throne." (The period is inside the quotation marks.)
   "None of the solutions is correct," said the professor. (The comma is inside the quotation marks.)

2. **To mark language that a writer has borrowed from another source:**
   The dictionary defines *gossip* as a "trivial rumor of a personal nature," but I would add that it is usually malicious.
   This research concludes that there was "no real reason to expect this computer software program to produce good results with high school students."

3. **To indicate when a word or phrase is being used in a special way:**
   The king believed himself to be the leader of a democracy, so he allowed the prisoner to choose his method of dying. According to the king, allowing this kind of "democracy" showed that he was indeed a good ruler.

Semicolons

The function of a semicolon is similar to that of a period. However, a semicolon suggests a stronger relationship between the sentences.

Joey loves to play tennis. He has been playing since he was ten years old.
Joey loves to play tennis; he has been playing since he was ten years old.

Both sentence pairs are correct. Notice that *he* is not capitalized in the second example.

A semicolon is often used with transition words like *however, therefore,* and *in addition.*

The price of gas is increasing; **therefore**, more people are taking public transportation.

In parts of Africa, elephants are being killed for their ivory tusks; **in addition**, rhinos are being hunted for their horns.

SENTENCE TYPES

English has three types of sentences: simple, compound, and complex. These labels indicate how the information in a sentence is organized, not how difficult the content is. Always try to vary the type of sentences you use in your writing.

Simple Sentences

Simple sentences usually contain one subject and one verb.

S   V
Children love electronic devices.

V   S   V
Does this sound like a normal routine?

Sometimes simple sentences can contain more than one subject or verb.

S   S   V
Brazil and the United States are large countries.

S   V   V
Brazil is in South America and has a large population.

Compound Sentences

coordinating conjunction

Compound sentences are usually made up of two simple sentences (independent clauses). The two sentences are connected with a coordinating conjunction such as *and, but, or, yet, so,* and *for.*

A comma is used before the coordinating conjunction.

Megan studied hard, **but** she did not pass the final test.

More and more people are shopping online, **so** many stores have been forced to close.

The administration will use the funds to purchase new computers, **or** it will use them to remodel the school cafeteria.

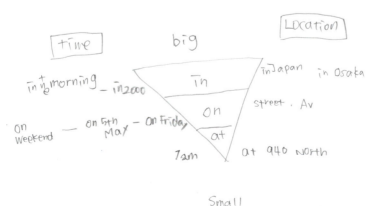

Complex Sentences

Complex sentences contain one independent clause and at least one dependent clause. In most complex sentences, the dependent clause is an adverb clause. (Other complex sentences have dependent adjective clauses or dependent noun clauses.)

Adverb clauses begin with subordinating conjunctions, such as *while*, *although*, *because*, and *if*.

Study the examples below. The adverb clauses are underlined, and the subordinating conjunctions are boldfaced. Notice that the subordinating conjunctions are part of the dependent clauses.

independent clause   *dependent clause*

The hurricane struck **while** we were at the mall.

dependent clause   *independent clause*

After the president gave his speech, he answered the reporters' questions.

Dependent clauses must be attached to an independent clause. They cannot stand alone as a sentence. If they are not attached to another sentence, they are called fragments, or incomplete sentences. Look at these examples:

Fragment: After the president gave his speech.

Complete Sentence: After the president gave his speech, he answered the questions.

Fragment: Although every citizen is entitled to vote.

Complete Sentence: Although every citizen is entitled to vote, many do not.

Fragment: If the election results are close.

Complete Sentence: If the election results are close, there may have to be a recount.

Subordinary conjonction

CONNECTORS

Using connectors will help your ideas flow. Three types of connectors are coordinating conjunctions, subordinating conjunctions, and transitions.

Coordinating Conjunctions

Coordinating conjunctions join two independent clauses to form a compound sentence. Use a comma before a coordinating conjunction in a compound sentence.

Independent clause, + coordinating + independent clause.
conjunction

The exam was extremely difficult, **but** all of the students received a passing score.

Subordinating Conjunctions

Subordinating conjunctions introduce a dependent clause in a complex sentence.

When a dependent clause begins a sentence, use a comma to separate it from the independent clause.

Dependent clause, + independent clause.

Although the exam was extremely difficult, all of the students received a passing score.

Subordinating conjunction

When a dependent clause comes after an independent clause, no comma is used.

Independent clause + dependent clause.

All of the students received a passing score **although** the exam was extremely difficult.

subordinating conjunction

Transition Words

Transition words show the relationship between ideas in sentences. A transition followed by a comma can begin a sentence.

Independent clause. Transition, independent clause.

The exam was extremely difficult. **However**, all of the students received a passing score.

A transition word followed by a comma can also come after a semicolon. Notice that in the independent clause that follows the semicolon, the first word is not capitalized.

Independent clause; transition, independent clause.

The exam was extremely difficult; **however**, all of the students received a passing score.

Here is a chart summarizing kinds of connectors and their purpose.

PURPOSE	COORDINATING CONJUNCTIONS	SUBORDINATING CONJUNCTIONS	TRANSITIONS
To give an example			For example, To illustrate, Specifically, In particular,
To add information	and		In addition, Moreover, Furthermore,
To signal a comparison			Similarly, Likewise, In the same way,
To signal a contrast	but yet	while although	In contrast, However, On the other hand, Conversely, Instead,
To signal a refutation		although even though	On the contrary, Nevertheless, However, Even so,
To emphasize			In fact, Actually,
To clarify			In other words, In simpler words, More simply,
To give a reason/ cause	for	because since	
To show a result	so		As a result, As a consequence, Consequently, Therefore, Thus,
To show time relationships		after as soon as before when while until since whenever as	Afterward, First, Second, Next, Then Finally, Subsequently, Meanwhile, In the meantime,
To signal a condition		if even if unless provided that when	
To signal a purpose		so that in order that	
To signal a choice	or		
To signal a conclusion			In conclusion, To summarize, As we have seen, In brief, To sum up,

USEFUL WORDS AND PHRASES

COMPARING	
Comparative adjective	New York is *larger than* Rhode Island.
Comparative adverb	A jet flies *faster than* a helicopter.
In comparison,	Canada has provinces. **In comparison,** Brazil has states.
Compared to Similar to Like	**Compared to** these roses, those roses last a long time.
Both … and	**Both model planes and** real planes have similar controls.
Likewise, Similarly,	Students spend hours each day developing their language skills to enhance their writing. **Likewise,** ballerinas spend countless hours in the gym each week increasing their accuracy and endurance.

CONTRASTING	
In contrast,	Algeria is a very large country. **In contrast,** the U.A.E. is very small.
Contrasted with In contrast to	**In contrast to** Chicago, Miami has only two seasons: a very mild winter and a very long summer.
Although Even though Though	**Though** London in 1900 was quite different from London in 2000 in many ways, important similarities existed in population, technology, and transportation.
Unlike	**Unlike** Chicago, the problem in Miami is not the cold but rather the heat.
However,	Canada has provinces. **However,** Brazil has states.
On the one hand, On the other hand,	**On the one hand,** Maggie loved to travel. **On the other hand,** she hated to be away from her home.

SHOWING CAUSE AND EFFECT

Because Since	**Because** their races are longer, distance runners need to be mentally strong.
cause lead to result in	An earthquake **can cause** tidal waves and massive destruction.
As a result of Because of	**Because of** the economic sanctions, the unemployment rate rose.
Therefore, As a result,	Markets fell. **Therefore,** millions of people lost their life savings.

STATING AN OPINION

I believe / think / feel / agree / that	**I believe that** using electronic devices on a plane should be allowed.
In my opinion / view / experience,	**In my opinion,** talking on a cell phone in a movie theater is extremely rude.
For this reason,	**For this reason,** voters should not pass this law.
There are many benefits / advantages / disadvantages to / of	**There are many benefits to** swimming every day.

ARGUING

It is important to remember that	**It is important to remember that** school uniforms would only be worn during school hours.
According to a recent survey,	**According to a recent survey,** the biggest fear of most people is public speaking.
For these reasons,	**For these reasons,** public schools should require uniforms.
Without a doubt,	**Without a doubt,** students ought to learn a foreign language.

GIVING A COUNTERARGUMENT

Proponents / Opponents may say	**Opponents** of uniforms **say** that students who wear uniforms cannot express their individuality. However, I argue that there are many other ways to express one's individuality.
One could argue that, but	**One could argue that** working for a small company is very exciting**, but** it can also be more stressful than a job in a large company.
Some people believe that	**Some people believe that** nuclear energy is the way of the future. We, on the other hand, believe that using nuclear energy has risks.
Although it is true that	**Although it is true that** taking online classes can be convenient, it is difficult for many students to stay on task.

AVOIDING PLAGIARISM

When writing a paragraph or an essay, you should use you own words for the most part. Sometimes, however, you may want to use ideas that you have read in a book, in an article, on a website, or that you have heard in a speech. It can make the paragraph or essay more interesting, more factual, or more relevant to the reader. For example, if you are writing a paragraph about a recent election, you may want to use a quotation from a politician. In this case, you must indicate that the words are not your own, but that they come from someone else. Indicating that your words are not original is called **citing**. In academic writing, it is necessary to cite all sources of information that are not original.

If the information does not come from your head, it must be cited. If you do not—whether intentionally or unintentionally—give credit to the original author, you are **plagiarizing**, or stealing, someone else's words. This is academic theft, and most institutions take it very seriously.

To avoid plagiarism, it is important to use quotes or a paraphrase, include an in-text citation, and add a reference or bibliography at the end of your writing.

Using Quotes

Quotations are used when you want to keep the source's exact words. A common way to introduce a quote is with the phrase *According to*. There are also several verbs that can be used to introduce someone else's ideas.

argue	describe	insist	predict	say
claim	find	point out	report	state

Here are three different examples of quoting a sentence from a text.

Original*: There is absolutely no empirical evidence—quantitative or qualitative —to support the familiar notion that monolingual dictionaries are better than bilingual dictionaries for understanding and learning L2.

Quote 1: According to Folse (2004), "There is absolutely no empirical evidence—quantitative or qualitative—to support the familiar notion that monolingual dictionaries are better than bilingual dictionaries for understanding and learning L2."

Quote 2: And while instructors continue to push for monolingual dictionaries, "there is absolutely no empirical evidence—quantitative or qualitative—to support the familiar notion that monolingual dictionaries are better than bilingual dictionaries for understanding and learning L2." (Folse, 2004).

Quote 3: As Folse points out, "There is absolutely no empirical evidence – quantitative or qualitative—to support the familiar notion that monolingual dictionaries are better than bilingual dictionaries for understanding and learning L2" (2004).

Note that brief in-text citations in the body of your work are appropriate for quotes like these. But you must also list the complete source at the end of your work.

*Folse, Keith. *Vocabulary Myths: Applying Second Language Research to Classroom Teaching*. University of Michigan Press, 2004.

Paraphrasing

Sometimes you may want to paraphrase or summarize outside information. In this case, the same rules still hold true. If the ideas are not yours, they must be cited. When you paraphrase, you retain the original ideas but use your own words. Your paraphrase should not be too close to the original, or it is considered plagiarism. Notice how this is done in the examples below.

Original*:   Every year, the town of Vinci, Italy, receives as many as 500,000 visitors—people coming in search of its most famous son, Leonardo.

Paraphrase: Although a small town, Vinci is visited by many tourists because it is the birthplace of Leonardo da Vinci (Herrick, 2009).

Original*:   This quiet, unimposing hill town is relatively unchanged from the time of Leonardo.

Paraphrase: Herrick (2009) explains that even after 500 years, the town of Vinci has remained much the same.

*Herrick, Troy. "*Vinci: A Visit to Leonardo's Home Town.*" Offbeat Travel, Updated January 5, 2016, www.offbeattravel.com/vinci-italy-davinci-home.html.

Bibliography

At the end of your paragraph or essay, you must list the sources you used. There are many types of citation styles. Among the most commonly used are APA, Chicago, and MLA, with MLA being the most common in the liberal arts and humanities fields Ask your instructor which one you should use. The bibliography, or MLA Works Cited page at the end of your work, should include complete sources for all quotes and paraphrases, but also any source that helped you develop your work. Here are some guidelines for referencing different works using MLA:

SOURCE	INFORMATION TO INCLUDE	EXAMPLE
Book	Last name of author, first name. *Title of Book.* Publisher, year of publication.	Folse, Keith. *Vocabulary Myths: Applying Second Language Research to Classroom Teaching.* University of Michigan Press, 2004.
Online Article	Last name of author, first name (if there is one). "*Title of Web Page.*" Title of Website, Publisher, Date published, URL.	"*Becoming a Vegetarian.*" Harvard Health Publishing, Harvard University, October 2009, updated December 4, 2017, www.health.harvard.edu/staying-healthy/becoming-a-vegetarian (Note that you should remove http:// and https:// from the URL.)
Website	Last name of author, first name (if there is one). "*Title of Web Page.*" Title of Website, Publisher, Date published (if given), URL.	"*The Complete Guide to MLA & Citations.*" Citation Machine, a Chegg Service, Study Break Media, www.citationmachine.net/mla/cite-a-website.
Newspaper	Last name of author, first name. "Title of Article." *Name of Newspaper*, Date, page numbers.	Smith, Steven. "What To Do in Case of Emergencies." *USA Today*, December 13, 2008, 2–3.

TEST TAKING TIPS

Before Writing

- Before you begin writing, make sure that you understand the assignment. Underline key words in the writing prompt. Look back at the key words as you write to be sure you are answering the question correctly and staying on topic.
- Take five minutes to plan before you start writing. First, list out all the ideas you have about the topic. Then think about which ideas have the best supporting examples or ideas. Use this information to choose your main idea(s). Circle the supporting information you want to include. Cross out other information.
- Organize your ideas before you write. Review the list you have created. Place a number next to each idea, from most important to least important. In this way, if you do not have enough time to complete your writing, you will be sure that the most relevant information will be included in your essay.

While Writing

For Paragraphs

- Be sure that your topic sentence has a clear and accurate controlling idea. Remember that your topic sentence guides your paragraph. If the topic sentence is not clear, the reader will have difficulty following your supporting ideas.
- It is important for your writing to look like a paragraph. Be sure to indent the first sentence. Write the rest of the sentences from margin to margin. Leave an appropriate amount of space after your periods. These small details make your paragraph easier to read and understand.

For Essays

- Be sure that your thesis statement responds to the prompt and expresses your main idea. The thesis may also include your points of development. Remember that if your thesis statement is not clear, the reader will have difficulty following the supporting ideas in the body paragraphs.
- Readers will pay special attention to the last paragraph of your essay, so take two or three minutes to check it before you submit it. Make sure your concluding paragraph restates information in the introduction paragraph and offers a suggestion, gives an opinion, asks a question, or makes a prediction.

For Either Paragraphs or Essays

- Do not write more than is requested. If the assignment asks for a 150-word response, be sure that your writing response comes close to that. Students do not get extra points for writing more than what is required.
- If you are using a word processor, choose a font that is academic and clear like Times New Roman or Calibri. Choose an appropriate point size like 12. Use double space or one and a half space so that it is easier to read. Remember to indent paragraphs and leave a space between sentences.

- Once you pick a side (agree or disagree), include only the ideas that support that side. Sometimes you may have ideas for both sides. If this happens, choose the side that is easier for you to write about. If you do not have an opinion, choose the side that you can write about most easily, even if you do not believe in it. You receive points for your writing skill, not your personal beliefs.

Word Choice

- Avoid using words such as *always*, *never*, *all*, and *none*. You cannot give enough proof for these words. Instead, use hedging words such as *probably*, *often*, *most*, *many*, *almost never*, and *almost none*. The modals *may*, *might*, and *could* are also used for hedging.
- Avoid using general or vague vocabulary. Words such as *nice*, *good*, and *very* can often be changed to more specific terms, such as *friendly*, *fabulous*, and *incredibly*. Be more specific in your word choice.
- Avoid conversational or informal language in academic writing.

Development

- Avoid information that is too general. When possible, give specific examples or data. Good writers want to show that they have thought about the subject and provide interesting and specific information in their writing.

After Writing

- Leave time to proofread your paragraph or essay. Check for subject-verb agreement, correct use of commas and end punctuation, and for clear ideas that all relate to the topic sentence (paragraphs) or thesis statement (essay).
- Check for informal language such as contractions or slang. These do not belong in academic writing.

Managing Time

- It is common to run out of time at the end of a writing test. Once you have written your introduction and the body paragraphs, check your remaining time. Then read through what you have written to check for the clarity of your ideas. If you are running out of time, write a very brief conclusion.

PEER EDITING FORMS

Peer Editing Form for Outlines

Reader: _____ Date: _____

1. What is the purpose of the essay?

   _____

2. What is the thesis statement?

   _____

3. What are the main points of development?

   _____

   _____

   _____

4. How many paragraphs are going to be in the essay?

   _____

   _____

   _____

5. Do you have any questions about the outline?   ☐ Yes   ☐ No

   If yes, write them here: _____

Peer Editing Form 1

Reader: _____ Date: _____

1. What is the topic of the paragraph? _____

2. What is the topic sentence? _____

3. Does the topic sentence have a controlling idea? ☐ Yes ☐ No

   Write it and/or suggest one. _____

   _____

4. Do all the supporting sentences relate to the topic sentence and controlling idea?

   ☐ Yes ☐ No

   If no, explain. _____

   _____

5. Does the paragraph have a concluding sentence? ☐ Yes ☐ No

   Write it and/or suggest one. _____

   _____

6. Are all the nouns in the correct form – singular or plural? ☐ Yes ☐ No

7. What do you like best about this paragraph?

   _____

   _____

8. Is there any place where you want more information? ☐ Yes ☐ No

   If yes, where? _____

Peer Editing Form 2

Reader: _____ Date: _____

1. What is the topic of the paragraph? _____

2. What is the topic sentence? _____

3. Does the topic sentence have a controlling idea? ☐ Yes ☐ No

   Write it and/or suggest one. _____

   _____

4. Do all the supporting sentences relate to the topic sentence and controlling idea?

   ☐ Yes ☐ No

   If no, explain. _____

   _____

5. Does the paragraph have a concluding sentence? ☐ Yes ☐ No

   Write it and/or suggest one. _____

6. Are transitional words and phrases correctly used? ☐ Yes ☐ No

   If no, explain. _____

   _____

7. What do you like best about this paragraph? _____

   _____

8. Is there any place where you want more information? ☐ Yes ☐ No

   If yes, where? _____

Peer Editing Form 3

Reader: _____ Date: _____

1. What is the topic sentence? _____

2. Does the topic sentence have an effective controlling idea? ☐ Yes ☐ No

   If yes, write it here: _____

   If no, explain. _____

3. What is the purpose of the paragraph? Check one.

   a. To classify   c. to explain causes and effects

   b. To compare   d. to present a problem and solution

4. Do all the supporting sentences relate to the topic sentence and controlling idea?

   ☐ Yes ☐ No

   If no, explain. _____

   _____

5. Does the paragraph have a logical concluding sentence? ☐ Yes ☐ No

   If yes, write it here. _____

   If no, explain. _____

6. What do you like best about this paragraph? _____

   _____

7. Is there any place where you want more information? ☐ Yes ☐ No

   If yes, where? _____

Peer Editing Form 4

Reader: _____ Date: _____

1. What is the purpose of the essay?

   _____

   _____

2. Does the introduction have an effective hook?   ☐ Yes   ☐ No

   _____

   _____

   Write it and/or suggest another one. _____

3. Is the thesis statement clear?   ☐ Yes   ☐ No

   _____

   If yes, what is it? _____

   _____

4. Does each body paragraph have a topic sentence related to the thesis?   ☐ Yes   ☐ No

   If no, explain. _____

   _____

5. Does the essay have a logical conclusion?   ☐ Yes   ☐ No

   Write it and/or suggest one. _____

   _____

6. What do you like best about this essay? _____

   _____

Peer Editing Form 5

Reader: _____ Date: _____

1. Does the essay focus on causes or effects? _____

2. Does the introduction have an effective hook?   ☐ Yes   ☐ No

   Write it and/or suggest one. _____

   _____

3. Is the thesis statement clear?   ☐ Yes   ☐ No

   If yes, what is it? _____

   _____

4. Does each body paragraph have a topic sentence related to the thesis?   ☐ Yes   ☐ No

   If no, explain. _____

   _____

5. Does the essay have a logical conclusion?   ☐ Yes   ☐ No

   Write it and/or suggest one. _____

   _____

6. What do you like best about this essay? _____

   _____

7. Is there any place where you would like more information?   ☐ Yes   ☐ No

   If yes, where? _____

   _____

Peer Editing Form 6

Reader: _____ Date: _____

1. How is the comparison essay organized: block method ☐   point-by point method ☐

2. Does the introduction have an effective hook?   ☐ Yes   ☐ No

   Write it and/or suggest one. _____

   _____

3. Is the thesis statement clear?   ☐ Yes   ☐ No

   If yes, what is it? _____

   _____

4. Does each body paragraph have a topic sentence related to the thesis?   ☐ Yes   ☐ No

   If no, explain. _____

   _____

5. Does the essay have a logical conclusion?   ☐ Yes   ☐ No

   Write it and/or suggest one. _____

   _____

6. What do you like best about this essay? _____

   _____

7. Is there any place where you would like more information?   ☐ Yes   ☐ No

   If yes, where? _____

   _____

Peer Editing Form 7

Reader: _____ Date: _____

1. What problem does this essay discuss? _____

_____

2. Does the writer focus on one solution or multiple solutions? _____

3. Is the thesis statement clear? ☐ Yes ☐ No

Write it and/or suggest one. _____

_____

4. Does each body paragraph have a topic sentence related to the thesis? ☐ Yes ☐ No

If no, explain. _____

_____

5. Does the essay have a logical conclusion? ☐ Yes ☐ No

Write it and/or suggest one. _____

_____

6. Does the essay include a variety of sentence types? ☐ Yes ☐ No

7. Is there any place where you would like more information? ☐ Yes ☐ No

If yes, where? _____

_____

VOCABULARY INDEX

Word	Page	CEFR† Level	Word	Page	CEFR† Level	Word	Page	CEFR† Level
range from*	87	B2	severe	138	B2	task*	162	B2
react*	93	B2	shrink	60	B2	tend to	10	B2
recommendation	10	B2	signal	41	B2	terrifying	162	B2
reduce	46	B1	significantly*	34	B2	threat	138	B2
regardless of	10	C1	simply	114	B2	throughout	6	B2
rehearse	87	C1	skip*	93	B2	tie up	46	B2
release*	41	B2	slight	162	B2	transform*	122	B2
rely on*	22	B2	solo	93	B2	tremendous	120	B2
remarkably	146	C1	specific*	114	B2	unbearable	138	B2
replacement*	87	B2	spin	146	C1	unique*	87	B2
resident*	138	B2	stimulate	41	B2	unlike	43	B2
result in	120	B2	strategy*	69	B2	urban	138	B2
retention*	169	C2	substance	34	B2	visual*	87	B2
risk	122	B2	sufficient*	162	B2	whichever*	87	B2
satisfying	122	B2	survey*	162	B2			

Every unit in *Great Writing* highlights key academic vocabulary, indicated by **AW**. These words have been selected using the Academic Word List (Coxhead, 2000) and the New Academic Word List (Browne, C., Culligan, B. & Phillips, J., 2013).

*These words are on the AWL or NAWL.

†Vocabulary was also chosen based on levels of The Common European Framework of Reference for Languages (CEFR). CEFR is an international standard for describing language proficiency. *Great Writing 3* is most appropriate for students at CEFR level B2.

The target vocabulary is at the CEFR levels as shown.

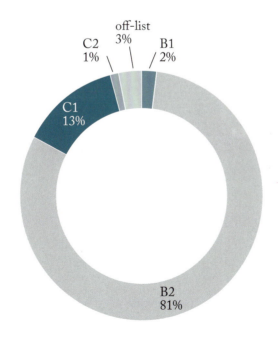

INDEX